Purr-fect Patchwork

16 Appliqué, Embroidery & Quilt Projects for Modern Cat People

Pamela Jane Morgan

stash BOOKS.

an imprint of C&T Publishing

Text, photography, and artwork copyright © 2021 by Pamela Jane Morgan

Artwork copyright © 2021 by C&T Publishing, Inc.

Publisher: Amy Barrett-Daffin

Creative Director: Gailen Runge

Acquisitions Editor: Roxane Cerda

Managing Editor: Liz Aneloski

Editor: Kathryn Patterson

Technical Editor: Helen Frost

Cover/Book Designer: April Mostek

Production Coordinator: Zinnia Heinzmann

Production Editor: Jennifer Warren

Illustrators: Pamela Jane Morgan and Aliza Shalit

Photo Assistants: Lauren Herberg and Gabriel Martinez

Photography by Pamela Jane Morgan, unless otherwise noted

Published by Stash Books, an imprint of C&T Publishing, Inc., P.O. Box 1456, Lafayette, CA 94549

Library of Congress Cataloging-in-Publication Data

Names: Morgan, Pamela Jane, 1984- author.

Title: Purr-fect patchwork : 16 appliqué, embroidery & quilt projects for modern cat people / Pamela Jane Morgan.

Description: Lafayette, CA : Stash Books, an imprint of C&T Publishing, [2021]

Identifiers: LCCN 2020056860 | ISBN 9781644030974 (trade paperback) | ISBN 9781644030981 (ebook)

Subjects: LCSH: Patchwork--Patterns. | Quilting--Patterns. | Appliqué--Patterns. | Decoration and ornament--Animal forms.

Classification: LCC TT835 .M6813 2021 | DDC 746.46/041--dc23

LC record available at https://lccn.loc.gov/2020056860

Printed in China

10 9 8 7 6 5 4 3 2 1

Dedication

For Susanne Woods. Your influence in the quilting world
was immeasurable. You will be forever missed.

Acknowledgments First and foremost, I must thank my husband for his unwavering support and encouragement, and for having faith in me when I didn't have faith in myself. I love you. You are my rock. Charisma, thank you for always being my cheerleader, for helping me piece and quilt several of the quilts in this book, and for always being there to talk me down when I was busy being a hot mess. Thank you, Sherri, for always being so encouraging and having so much faith in my work. Also, thank you for making the alternate colorway of *Chasing Dreams*. Amanda, I am so grateful for all the gorgeous florals you arranged for my book and for always being on the lookout for the best vintage props! Thank you to everyone who helped make sure that *Purr-fect Patchwork* was not wasted when we unexpectedly lost Susanne. I will be forever grateful. A big thanks to my dear friend Jana for helping me finish piecing, for giving me the drive to get stuff done, and for making me feel way cooler than I actually am. I couldn't have finished this book without your help. And finally, thanks to everyone at C&T Publishing for making this book happen and for being so great to work with.

Contents

PROJECTS
36

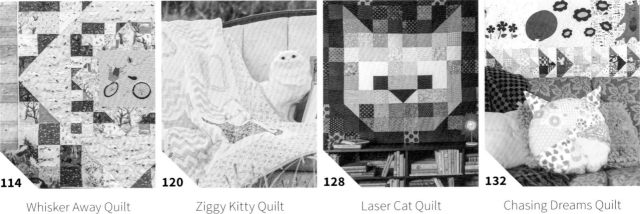

Introduction

Hey all you cool cats and kittens! I am here to tell you that I am a cat lady. And I am not ashamed of it. I am not a spinster with nothing in her life but her cats. In fact, I'm quite the opposite: I'm married to a wonderful man and have four amazing children and a busy, robust life. And yet it is cats that I find to be my greatest source of inspiration. I am not alone!

The Love of Cats Is Inspiring

Many famous artists, actors, singers, and writers are or have been cat lovers. Freddie Mercury, arguably one of the greatest singer-songwriters of all time, was a cat lover. It is said that he spoke on the phone to his cats when he was touring. His liner notes in one of his albums were dedicated to his cats. He even wrote a song, "Delilah," about one of his favorite cats.

Ernest Hemingway, a Nobel Prize–winning author, was a known cat lover. At one point, he was the owner of more than 50 cats, saying that he loved nothing more than the feeling of cats underfoot. He began collecting polydactyl cats, cats born with more than the usual number of toes, which he believed to be good luck. His Key West home is now a museum and is home to many cats who are purportedly descendants of his first polydactyl cat.

Artists from Leonardo da Vinci to Georgia O'Keeffe to Pablo Picasso have all been cat lovers. Leonardo da Vinci has famous etchings of cats, including one which morphs into a dragon. Artist Andy Warhol created artwork based on his love of his cats. Georgia O'Keeffe and Frida Kahlo, among others, were famously photographed with their pet cats.

Love of cats among creatives is not limited to those of the past. Current musician Taylor Swift has credited her cats as her greatest inspiration. James Franco of *Spiderman* fame is rumored to be a cat lover. You can find cat lovers from rapper Snoop Dogg to actor Christopher Walken to pop sensation Katy Perry. A quick browse on the internet will reveal a multitude of material devoted to cats, everything from memes to comics to humorous videos. You will even find social media accounts owned by cats, who've become famous in their own right!

But why is it that the artistically minded and cats seem to find themselves intertwined? Do we find cats to be a muse of sorts? Or maybe their soothing nature and the sound of their purrs bring about a calm that inspires us to create. Perhaps it's their ability to express their emotions in a way that humans seem to be incapable of that we find so inspiring. Or their ability to move with a certain fluidity and grace that evades other members of the animal kingdom. Whatever the reason may be, it is my love of these magnificent creatures that led to the creation of this book.

"A cat has absolute emotional honesty; human beings, for one reason or another, may hide their feelings, but a cat does not."

ERNEST HEMINGWAY

Cat-Loving Quilters, Mew-nite!

The inexplicable link between cats and creativity is not lost on quilters.

I once had the opportunity to listen to famed quilter and fabric designer Tula Pink speak. It was just prior to the announcement of her fabric collection, Tabby Road. She had previously stated that she would never release a collection of fabric dedicated to a domesticated animal. But when she ultimately decided to design a line that was based on a house pet, it could only be the very best pet—a cat.

Quilters are very much a community, as are cat lovers. Instagram seems to be a popular hub for quilters and cat lovers alike. Browsing the hashtag #catsonquilts yields thousands of images of our furry friends taking comfort in our creations. I recently discovered a Facebook group called Sewing with Cats that is dedicated to sharing photos of our beloved pets taking over our creative spaces.

Let's continue to grow our community of quilting cat lovers! Don't forget to share pictures of your projects from this book, using **#catsonquilts** and **#purrfectpatchwork**. Like the popular hashtag #quiltyfriendsarethebest says, quilty friends really are the best—whether human or feline.

Techniques

If I were to pick a term to describe my style, it would have to be maximalist. *I believe that the cool cats refer to it as being* extra. *My projects are loaded with color, print, texture, and a wide variety of techniques. In short, I like to try* all the things*! In this section, I'll teach you how to do all the things so your quilts and projects can be extra, just like mine. Don't worry—I won't call you a copycat.*

Piecing Purr-fection

What's more extra than "purr-fection"? Follow these tips to help you piece like a "purr-fessional."

Stitch-and-Flip Piecing

Where there are pointy cat ears, there are bound to be half-square triangles. I find the most precise way to make half-square triangles is the stitch-and-flip technique. While there is some fabric waste in this technique, it improves accuracy because there is no sewing along raw bias edges, which can easily distort a block. The steps to this technique are simple.

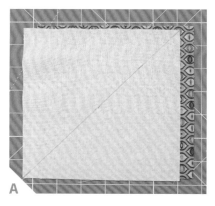

A

1 Draw a diagonal line on the wrong side of a fabric square. Align the square, right sides together, with another square or a rectangle. **A**

2 Stitch on the drawn line. Trim, leaving a ¼″ seam allowance. **B**

3 Flip the block open and press. **C**

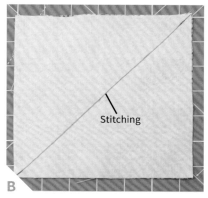

Stitching

B

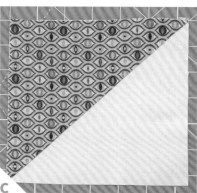

C

Two-at-a-Time Stitch-and-Flip Piecing

Some patterns call for 2 half-square triangles to be made from a pair of squares. This can also be accomplished using the stitch-and-flip technique.

1 Draw a diagonal line on the wrong side of a fabric square. Place atop another square, right sides together. **D**

2 Stitch ¼˝ from either side of the marked line. **E**

3 Cut on the marked line. **F**

4 Flip the blocks open and press. **G**

Stitch–and–Flip Flying Geese

Some projects like my *Ziggy Kitty Quilt* (page 120) include Flying Geese blocks. Making Flying Geese using the stitch-and-flip technique is a breeze!

1 Each Flying Geese unit is made up of 1 rectangle and 2 squares. Draw a diagonal line on the wrong side of both squares. **H**

2 With right sides facing, layer a marked square with one end of the rectangle. Sew on the drawn line. **I**

3 Trim, leaving a ¼˝ seam allowance. Press the triangle open. **J**

4 Repeat with the second square on the opposite end of the rectangle. **K**

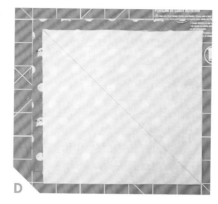

D

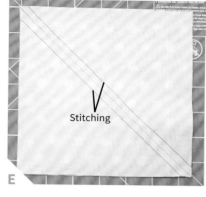

Stitching

E

F

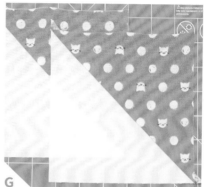

G

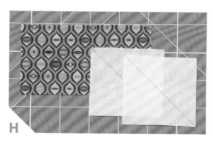

H

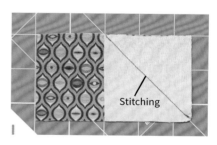

Stitching

I

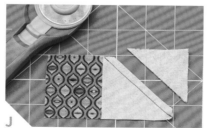

J

K

Square It Up

Many of the half-square triangle blocks in this book include excess material and require trimming. Why, you ask? The mathematical formula for creating half-square triangles typically leads to cuts that end in ⅛″ increments. In general, these are more difficult to cut accurately. And even when sewing very carefully, it can be difficult to sew a "purr-fectly" straight line. While there is, again, some waste involved, the ability to trim allows for all blocks to be cut to the same size and increases the likelihood of having "purr-fect" points.

1 Place the pressed half-square triangle block right side up on the cutting mat. **L**

2 Align the 45°-angle line on the ruler with the diagonal seam. Reposition the ruler so that a small amount of fabric extends beyond the edge of the ruler. Additionally, fabric should also extend beyond the trim line in other directions. **M**

TIP *If using a ruler other than the exact size of the block, use painter's tape or other colored, removable tape to mark the trim size on the ruler.*

3 Trim along both exposed edges. Rotate the block 180°. If necessary, reposition the ruler to expose the untrimmed edges, aligning the 45° angle with the diagonal seam, and square the edge of the ruler with the previously cut edges.

4 Trim the remaining edges so that the block is now cut to the desired size. **N**

TIP *A rotating cut mat and a square ruler in the same size as your trimmed half-square triangles are useful tools that will greatly speed up the trimming process.*

L

M

N

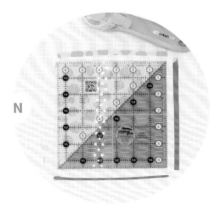

One Cat Leads to Another

Several of the full-size quilts featured in this book contain the same cat block. While there are variations in size, the basic construction is identical. For the sake of brevity, I will provide detailed instructions only once. The individual patterns will only include a labeled assembly diagram.

"One cat just leads to another."

ERNEST HEMINGWAY

THE CAT BODY

1 Draw a diagonal line on the wrong sides of 2 ear squares. Align right sides together with the bottom corners of a background rectangle. **O**

2 Sew along the drawn lines and trim the outside corners, leaving a ¼″ seam allowance. Press the triangles open. **P**

3 With right sides facing, layer the ear unit with the top edge of the body piece and sew together. **Q**

4 Draw a diagonal line on the wrong side of a background square. With right sides facing, layer with the bottom left corner of the body piece, paying attention to the direction of the diagonal line. **R**

5 Sew on the drawn line and trim, leaving a ¼″ seam allowance. Press the triangle open. **S**

Note **Steps 4 and 5 are eliminated in the print Kitty blocks in** *Ziggy Kitty* **(page 120).**

---

6 Draw a diagonal line on the wrong side of a background square. With right sides together, layer with the top corner of a middle-unit rectangle. Sew along the drawn line. Trim, leaving a ¼″ seam allowance. Press the triangle open. **T**

7 With right sides together, layer a background rectangle with the top edge of the pieced unit. Sew along the short edge. **U**

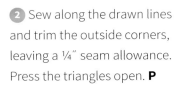

O 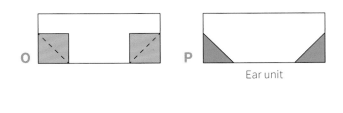 P

Ear unit

Q  R  S

Body unit

T 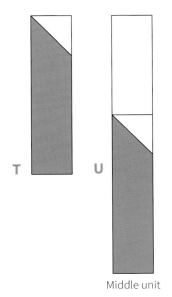 U

Middle unit

THE TAIL SECTIONS

1 Draw a diagonal line on the wrong side of 2 background squares. Layer right sides together with both corners of a tail top unit rectangle. Sew along the drawn lines. Trim, leaving a ¼″ seam allowance. Press the triangles open. **V**

2 With right sides together, layer a tail middle unit rectangle with the right edge of a background rectangle. Sew the long edges together. **W**

3 Draw a diagonal line on the wrong side of a background square. With right sides together, layer with the right corner of a tail bottom unit rectangle. Sew on the drawn line. Trim, leaving a ¼″ seam allowance. Press the triangle open. **X**

4 Assemble the tail unit as shown. **Y**

ASSEMBLE THE CAT

Sew the body unit, middle unit, and tail unit together. **Z**

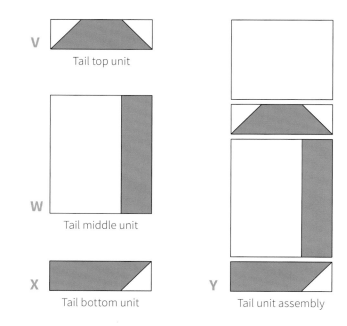

V

Tail top unit

W

Tail middle unit

X

Tail bottom unit

Y

Tail unit assembly

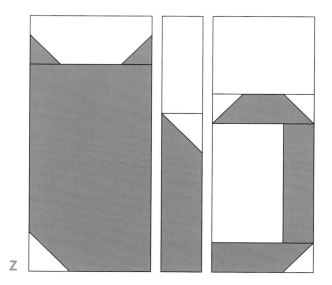

Z

Pressing Matters

There are different schools of thought when it comes to pressing quilt blocks. To steam or not to steam? Press seams to one side, or press them open? I personally don't like using steam. I think that it can create distortion, and it sometimes even shrinks my blocks. I use a hot, dry iron for most of my pressing needs.

For blocks with lots of bias seams or stubborn wrinkles, I use a homemade starch spray. I've tried many pressing sprays and starches, and I find this blend to be superior to any mass-produced product. It's also very inexpensive and lasts quite a while.

DIY pressing spray

To make your own pressing spray, you will need 1 gallon of distilled water, 1 bottle (750ml) of the cheapest vodka you can find (yes, you read that correctly), and ¼–½ cup of Sta-Flo Liquid Starch (by Purex). If desired, add a few drops of your favorite essential oil. (I use a combination of lemon, orange, and grapefruit oils.) Mix well. Pour into a fine mist spray bottle to use. Store the remaining mixture in the empty distilled water jug.

As far as how to press seams, it depends on the block. For tiny piecing and blocks where multiple seams meet in the same place, I suggest pressing seams open. This eliminates bulk, which overall leads to more accurate piecing. For blocks with simple seams, I suggest pressing toward the darker fabric. In my patterns, I give instructions for pressing that are appropriate for the specific block and/or pattern.

Best Practices for Tiny Patchwork

Some of the patterns in this book feature itty-bitty piecing. Where tiny piecing is involved, my personal preference is foundation paper piecing (FPP). For this reason, many of my patterns include paper-piecing foundations. However, many people find FPP to be very intimidating, so I'll share my tips for precision piecing tiny blocks the traditional way.

- **Check your ¼″ seam for accuracy.** Use a ¼″ patchwork foot, and double-check your seam allowances. If necessary, adjust your needle position to make sure you're sewing purr-fect ¼″ seams. It will make all the difference!

- **Use a short stitch length.** Set your stitch length to 1.8. A shorter stitch length will help keep your seams secure and the blocks from pulling apart.

- **Use an ultrafine pen.** For blocks that require you to sew along a drawn line, use the finest-point pen you can find. A difference as much as even a needle's width can cause distortion when it comes to tiny patchwork.

- **Press seams open.** For small patchwork, open seams are the way to go! Less bulk = greater precision.

Adding Hand Embroidery to Your Quilts

One of my favorite ways to add a little something extra to my projects is including hand embroidery designs, whether it be adding a few stitches to a motif that's present in a fabric collection or incorporating my own original designs. Many of the projects in this book feature my original designs. Feel free to use them as is or add some of your own designs.

Basic Embroidery Supplies

In this book, only a small smattering of embroidery is used, thus a limited number of supplies are needed. I will share with you what products are used in this book only. For more advanced embroidery projects, a wider variety of tools and supplies may be necessary.

NEEDLES

Choosing needles is a highly subjective process. Walk into a craft store and you can easily become overwhelmed by the variety of needles and brands. A simple solution is to try a few varieties, both of needle type and brand, and over time you will choose what works best for you. I use milliners (or straw) needles, embroidery needles, and chenille needles in a variety of sizes. My personal preference is Clover brand needles.

THREAD

All of the projects in this book were completed with either DMC 6-strand floss or DMC size 5 or 8 perle cotton. Both are available at just about any fabric or craft store and come in a multitude of colors.

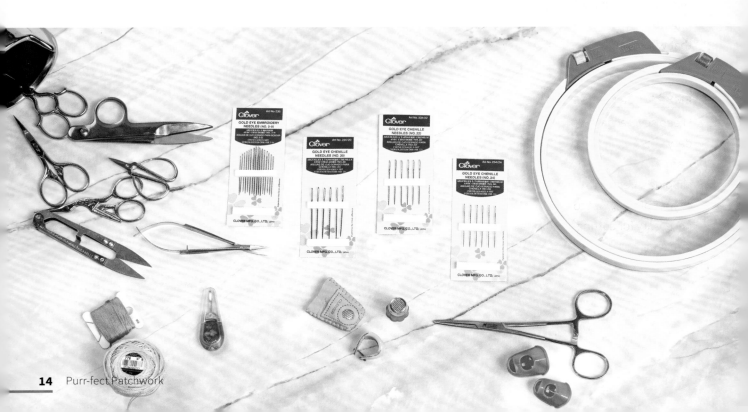

HOOPS

For adding embroidery to quilts, I prefer round plastic hoops and keep a variety of sizes on hand. I use plastic hoops when working on quilts because I feel that they cause less distortion, and there is less risk of snags than with traditional wooden hoops.

THIMBLES

There are many different kinds of thimbles, from traditional metal thimbles to leather thimbles to thimble pads that adhere to your fingertips. Experiment and find one that works for you. Your fingers will thank you.

EMBROIDERY SCISSORS

I keep several pairs of 4″ embroidery scissors handy at all times. A small, sharp point is vital for clipping thread close to the surface of your project, not to mention necessary for cutting lengths of thread to use for stitching.

Transferring Designs

According to an old proverb, there's more than one way to skin a cat. (Ew. Let's not *actually* do that, okay?) There's also more than one way to transfer designs to your projects. Different projects and substrates may require different methods of transfer.

USE A LIGHT SOURCE

One way to transfer the designs provided in this book is to use a light source to trace the design directly on to the fabric using a fine-tip pen, such as a Pigma Micron pen (permanent) or a FriXion pen (heat removable). Tape your design to a clean window and let the sunlight do its thing! A lightbox isn't absolutely necessary but can be a great tool to have handy for tracing when there isn't enough sunlight available to trace your design.

Pros: It can be as cheap as free if you're using a window.

Cons: You can only use a window when it's sunny. It only works with lightweight fabrics that already have an element of transparency.

IRON-ON TRANSFER PEN

Sulky makes an iron-on transfer pen that works well for transferring designs to wool and felt. Simply trace a design that is in reverse and transfer to your project by pressing with a hot dry iron.

Pros: The pen's ink is easily visible on wool and felt, whereas other transfer methods are not.

Cons: It's permanent, so you have to be very careful with placement.

PRINTABLE TRANSFER SHEETS

C&T Publishing makes a product called Wash-Away Stitch Stabilizer. Use a scanner and printer or photocopier to transfer embroidery designs directly onto the sheets. Then peel the top layer off, like a sticker, and place on the surface to be embroidered. Once the embroidery is completed, follow the package instructions to dissolve the product in water.

Pros: This is the most precise and easiest transfer method.

Cons: Using water to dissolve can sometimes distort quilt blocks. You run the risk of colors bleeding and have to wait for project to dry before continuing.

USE A STABILIZER

For quilts, I like to use SF101 Shape-Flex (by Pellon). It's a lightweight, woven iron-on interfacing. I like this product because the quilt remains soft and flexible. It will keep your blocks from becoming distorted while embroidering and will also keep any stray threads from showing through. To use, cut a piece slightly larger than your design on all sides. Press using a hot dry iron to the wrong side of the fabric. Then embroider the design. This will remain on your project permanently.

WORK IN GOOD LIGHTING

Make sure your workspace is well lit to reduce eye strain. If your room isn't well lit, purchase a small task lamp that clips onto your embroidery hoop or project.

TO HOOP OR NOT TO HOOP?

This is entirely based on personal preference. Some people have no problem embroidering without a hoop. Me? Not so much. Do what works for you. Either way, you'll likely have cats chasing your dangling threads.

USE A THREAD CONDITIONER

A good thread conditioner, such as Thread Magic, will help your thread glide through your fabric with ease and prevents tangles.

WORKING WITH MULTIPLE LAYERS

Sometimes when adding embroidery to quilts, you'll have to work through several layers of fabric and possibly seam allowances. Using a thimble can help take some of the burden off your fingertips. In some instances, you may have difficulty pulling a needle through your quilt top, in which case silicone needle pullers or even a hemostat (kind of like needle-nose pliers, but for sewists) can become your new BFFs.

Hand Embroidery Stitches

I've included a small selection of decorative stitches that are used throughout this book to add embellishment to your projects. Let these instructions be a starting point for your handwork journey. But beware! This doesn't even scratch the surface of hand embroidery stitches—there are entire books dedicated to the subject.

RUNNING STITCH

BACKSTITCH

STEM STITCH

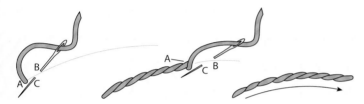

LAZY DAISY

CHAIN STITCH

BUTTONHOLE STITCH

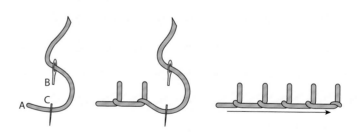

BUTTONHOLE PINWHEEL

FRENCH KNOT

COUCHING STITCH

Free-Motion Embroidery on Your Domestic Sewing Machine

Free-motion embroidery is a fun and easy way to give your quilt a hand-sketched appearance. The technique is similar to free-motion quilting, but instead of combining layers of fabric and batting with a free-flowing design, you're giving your appliqué motifs a "sketched" outline and a bit of character with contrasting thread.

Preparation

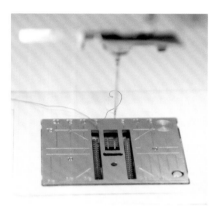 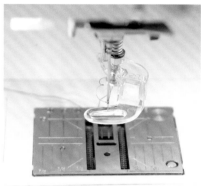 

Photo by Daniel Morgan

LOWER YOUR FEED DOGS

The vast majority of modern sewing machines have feed dogs that are capable of being lowered. Consult your owner's manual for instructions for your particular machine. If you are unable to lower your machine's feed dogs, cover them with several pieces of masking tape.

REPLACE YOUR PRESSER FOOT

Remove the standard presser foot from your sewing machine and replace with a darning foot or free-motion quilting foot.

HOOP YOUR FABRIC

Using an embroidery hoop that fits your entire motif, stretch the fabric taut over the outer hoop. Then push the inner hoop down over the top. Be sure to arrange so that fabric lies flat on the surface of your machine. Once you've arranged the hoops to your liking, tighten the set screw on the side of your hoop.

Stitching

PUT YOUR HOOP UNDER THE NEEDLE

Raise your needle and presser foot to their highest position. Carefully slide your hoop under your foot, taking precautions not to bend or damage your needle.

Note If your hoop is too high to pass under your needle and presser foot without causing damage, it may be necessary to remove both and replace them once the hoop is in position.

Photo by Daniel Morgan

PREPARE TO STITCH

Lower your needle into your fabric. Raise your needle, pulling the bobbin thread to the surface. Holding the 2 threads with light slack, take a few stitches in place to lock your stitches.

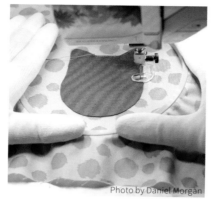
Photo by Daniel Morgan

TAKE YOUR FIRST STITCHES

Hold your hoop firmly and begin stitching, moving the hoop at a consistent speed to follow your design. When you've reached the end of your design, take a few locking stitches, similar to those done at the beginning. A pair of gloves designed for free-motion quilting, such as Machingers, can help you retain a firm grip on your project.

Practice Makes Purr-fect

Before stitching on your actual project, try a few practice motifs. This will help you get a feel for the speed you need to move your fabric under the needle. Longarm and free-motion quilters practice in much the same way. It helps build muscle memory. Essentially, your body remembers the movements you're making. With practice, you'll be able to achieve consistency in both speed and ability to follow a design.

Foundation Paper Piecing Like a Purr-fessional

It's no secret that I *love* foundation paper piecing! I love the precision and accuracy that foundation paper piecing affords makers. It's a worthwhile skill to have in your arsenal, yet many find it too challenging to learn. Here are some "pawesome" tips to make for a happy foundation paper-piecing experience!

Extra Investment

I'm not one for buying extra tools and gadgets unless I find them to be essential. I don't regret investing in an Add-A-Quarter ruler for my paper-piecing needs. Paired with a 4″ × 6″ piece of template plastic, it makes foundation paper piecing a breeze.

Additionally, there are some pawesome options on the market for copying your foundation templates. Try a few and see what works best for you!

The Best Foundation Paper–Piecing Tutorial in Hiss-tory

1 Copy or trace the foundation pattern to the desired paper. Cut the pattern from the paper, taking care not to trim the seam allowances. Choose a piece of fabric that is at least ¼″ larger than section 1 on all sides. Place the fabric piece, making sure to cover section 1 entirely on the wrong side of the foundation. **A**

TIP *Hold the foundation up to a sunny window, or use a lightbox if available, to ensure proper fabric placement.*

2 Using a washable fabric glue stick, such as the Sewline Fabric Glue Pen, secure the fabric to wrong side of the foundation.

3 Lay template plastic along the line between sections 1 and 2. Fold the paper, firmly pressing against the edge of the template plastic to create a nice crisp fold. **B**

4 Align the edge of your Add-A-Quarter ruler with the fold you just made. The Add-A-Quarter ruler has a small lip ¼″ from the edge. This lip catches the fold of your foundation paper, making it possible to trim a purr-fect ¼″ seam allowance. **C**

5 Trim a ¼″ seam allowance with your rotary cutter, using the Add-A-Quarter ruler as your guide. **D**

6 Begin section 2 by auditioning your fabric selection to ensure it will allow for at least ¼″ seam allowance on all sides. To check, align right sides together with section 1. Hold loosely against the seam allowance you've just trimmed. While holding along seam allowance, fold over to make sure that section 2 is covered.

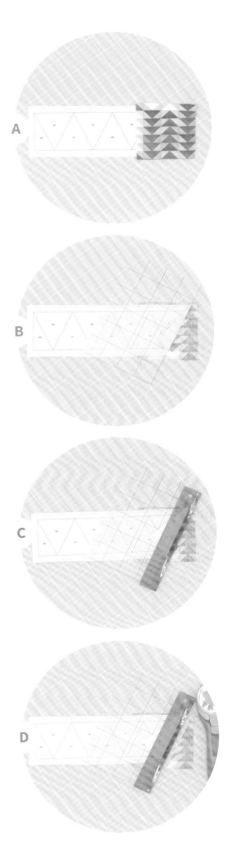

7 Pin section 2 on top of section 1, right sides together. Set your machine's stitch length to 1.8. Flip the foundation over and sew along the line between sections 1 and 2. **E**

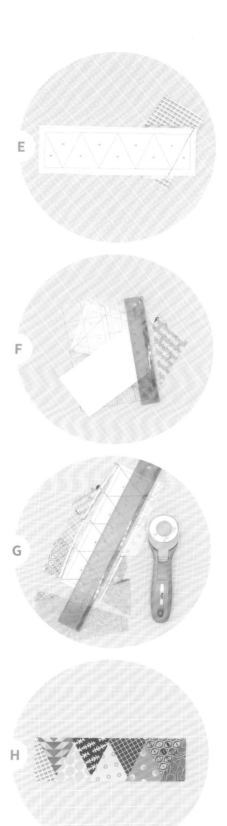

8 Using your template plastic and Add-A-Quarter ruler, fold the paper back along the sewn line so that the right sides of the paper are facing. Using your rotary cutter, trim leaving a ¼″ seam allowance. **F**

9 Press the fabric open with a hot, dry iron. Trim the seam allowance between sections 2 and 3 in the same manner as previous sections. Repeat these steps for all sections, working through the pattern in numerical order. Press open after each addition.

10 After completing all sections, trim the block to the correct size along the marked seam allowances. **G**

11 Upon the completion of the block, remove the paper by carefully tearing at each seam. Press again, this time using a pressing spray or starch to keep the block from stretching. **H**

JUST KEEP TRIMMING ...

Trim your seam allowances after the addition of each and every piece, including your first! Starting with a straight edge and an exact seam allowance makes it easier to estimate the size of your next piece. It also makes it easier to line up your next piece of fabric.

MADE A MISTAKE?

It happens to the best of us. Even the purr-fessionals! There's no need to start from scratch, though. Carefully remove the stitches from the section where you've made the mistake. Repair the foundation paper with transparent tape. Then continue where you left off. It's that simple!

Raw-Edge Appliqué

All of the appliqué projects in this book use raw-edge appliqué techniques, which add to their whimsical feel. If turned-edge appliqué is more your style, the designs will work for that purpose. However, note that all of the patterns included in this book are printed in reverse and that there aren't any instructions given for turned-edge appliqué. For additional resources, visit C&T Publishing's website (ctpub.com).

Transferring Motifs

All the appliqué motifs in this book are supplied in reverse for use with paper-backed fusible web. While the majority of the motifs in this book are made from wool or wool-blend felt, which do not fray, I still prefer to use an adhesive to hold them in place for stitching. The bonus is that it makes for easy transfer of the designs.

To transfer a motif, simply trace on to the paper side of your favorite paper-backed fusible web. Roughly cut the motif from the web, making sure not to use your good fabric-only scissors. Place paper side up on the wrong side of the fabric. Press with a hot, dry iron. Once cool, cut directly on the traced lines. Now you're ready to adhere the pieces to your foundation!

TIP *Try several fusible web products and find what works best for you. The ideal fusible web is sheer, lightweight, and has good adhesion without gumming up your needle. Recommendations: Soft Fuse (by Shades Textiles) or Wonder Fuse (by Clover). Whatever you choose, be sure to follow the manufacturer's instructions.*

TIP *Scissors with a small, sharp point and micro-serrated blades, such as Karen Kay Buckley's Perfect Scissors, are ideal for raw-edge appliqué. The micro-serrated blades decrease the likelihood of frayed edges.*

Placement

Some of the appliqué motifs used in this book are multilayered. For layered motifs, first fuse the top layers to the bottom layer of the motif, keeping the paper backing on the bottom layer until all the other layers have been fused.

Once all the motifs have been fused and cut out, press onto the appliqué foundation with a hot, dry iron. Hold the iron over each section of your motif for several seconds to allow for proper adhesion.

Refer to the layout diagram or quilt photo for the projects with appliqué for the correct placement of the motifs.

In most of the projects, the appliqué motifs are machine stitched. Several projects use a combination of hand and machine appliqué stitches. The combination of hand and machine stitching adds to the whimsy!

Hand Appliqué Stitches

HIDDEN WHIPSTITCH

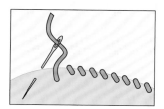

VISIBLE WHIPSTITCH

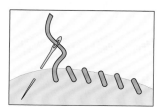

BLANKET STITCH

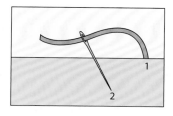 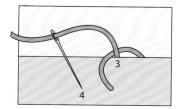 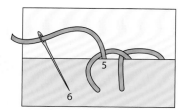

RUNNING STITCH

BACKSTITCH

Machine Appliqué Stitches

Most modern sewing machines come with a minimum of 7 or 8 stitch selections, and many higher-end machines feature a selection of purely decorative stitches as well. Experiment with stitches on your machine, as well as a variety of widths and lengths of each stitch, to see which best suit your style.

STRAIGHT STITCH

This is the basic sewing machine stitch. Stitch close (1/16″ to a scant 1/8″) to the raw edges of a fused motif. For some narrow motifs, such as flower stems or stripes on a bee, a single line of straight stitches is all that is necessary.

ZIGZAG STITCH

This is the traditional method for machine appliqué. Experiment with stitch width and length settings on your machine to find the look you prefer.

BLANKET OR BUTTONHOLE STITCH

Some older machines and more basic machines may not have this stitch. It happens to be one of my favorite looks for machine appliqué. It fits the whimsical feel of my designs without the extra time commitment of stitching by hand. It can be stitched with a matching thread for a more polished look or a contrasting thread to add an extra touch of whimsy. Either way, it's a great stitch to have.

TIP *A sewing machine with the capability of having the needle stop in the down position is helpful for machine appliqué. It is especially helpful when stitching around curves. Consult your machine's owners' manual to find out if your machine has this capability.*

Take It to Another Dimension

Some of the projects in this book are more dimensional than others. Here are my tips for making those shapely projects look like they were made by a purr-fessional.

Just a Little Off the Top

One of a cat's defining features is its pointy ears. It can be tricky to keep those points pointy when working with stuffing or foam interfacing. In all of the patterns with three-dimensional ears, I suggest that you trim the point, taking care not to cut too close to the stitching.

The ears, while inside out, will look similar to this:

Using your rotary cutter or a sharp pair of scissors, trim the point, leaving roughly an ⅛″ seam allowance. Eliminating some of the bulk will help maintain a nice, crisp point when turned right side out.

Learn to Love Your Curves

Inasmuch as we want to keep our points pointy, we want to keep our curves curvy as well. These best practices will help you master sewing curves in no time!

• Take it slow, and if possible, set your machine so that your needle stops in the down position. This makes it easier to pivot around curved pieces.

• The projects that include curved seams call for you to clip your seam allowance. Clipping notches in your seam allowance will afford your seams some give. Just be careful not to clip through your stitching.

Fancy Finishes

Some projects in this book have curved edges, which require a special finish—bias binding. At first glance, bias binding can seem intimidating. In actuality, it's no harder than making traditional binding. And, using this method, you'll only be required to sew 2 seams. Let's see how it's done!

Continuous Bias Binding

The scariest part of bias binding for many people is the math. For the purposes of this book, I've done the math for you. However, if math is your thing and you'd like to learn to calculate what size square you'll need for future projects, a quick internet or Pinterest search for "bias binding calculator" will reveal a multitude of tutorials.

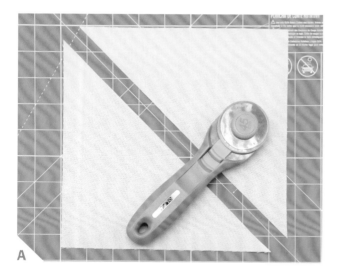

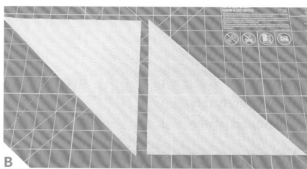

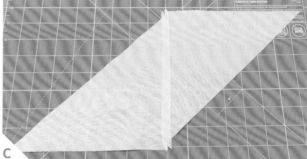

1 Begin by cutting the size square required for your project. Once you've got your square, cut it in half diagonally. **A**

2 Flip one-half of your cut square around to form a parallelogram. **B**

3 Join the 2 pieces of the parallelogram by stitching with a ¼″ seam allowance along the straight edge. Press the seam open. **C**

4 Using a fine-point marking tool, draw parallel lines spaced 2½″ apart on the wrong side of your fabric. **D**

Photos by Daniel Morgan

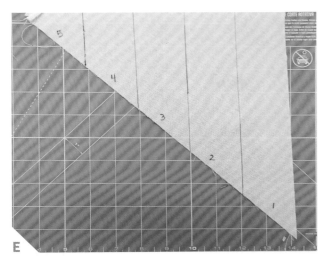

E

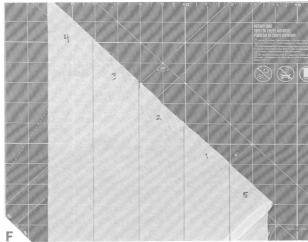

F

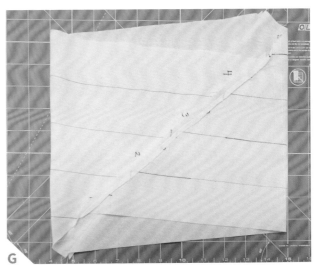

G

5 Beginning with the bottom right corner of your parallelogram, number the bottom of the strips you just drew, ending with the bottom left corner. **E**

6 Next, number the top half of your strips. Begin numbering in the top right corner, starting with the number in the bottom left corner. The second strip from the right will be labeled number one. From there, continue numbering as usual. **F**

7 Fold to create a rectangular tube. Match your numbered strips, starting with strip number 1. Pin on the drawn lines. Stitch using a ¼˝ seam allowance. Press the seams open. **G**

8 Cut along the lines in a spiral direction, working your way from the top of the tube to the bottom. You should end up with 1 continuous strip of bias binding. **H**

Once you've finished cutting your continuous strip of bias binding, proceed to bind your project as normal. It's that simple to create a fancy finish!

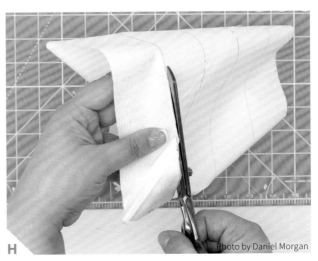

H

Photo by Daniel Morgan

Choosing Materials and Creating Texture

One of my favorite parts of the quilting process is experimentation with color, pattern, and texture. For some people, choosing materials and textures for their projects comes naturally. For others, it's more of a challenge. However, this skill can be learned, and we'll explore the process together!

Quilting Cottons

Quality 100% cotton fabrics are the most basic components of a quilter's toolkit. They are the foundation for most of the projects in this book and for quilting in general. Buyer beware, as not all cotton fabrics are created equal. There is a noticeable difference in quality between the fabric you'll find at your local quilt shop and what's available at large retail chains. A good rule of thumb when choosing quilting cottons is to buy the best quality fabric you can afford. If you're working with a limited budget, browse the clearance section at your local quilt shop. Chances are you'll find some great fabrics that are discounted to make way for new designs.

A Note About Fabric Availability The life cycle of a fabric collection is brief. While it may be tempting to try to recreate the projects *exactly* as they appear in this book, please note that many of the fabric collections featured will be long out of print by the date of publication. This may feel like a problem if you find selecting fabric to be a challenge. But a brief lesson on color theory will have you feeling confident in selecting your own fabrics. The Ultimate 3-in-1 Color Tool by Joen Wolfrom is an excellent resource, available from C&T Publishing (ctpub.com).

If you're still feeling stumped when it comes to fabric selection, here are a few more tips.

PRINTS OR SOLIDS?

Most quilters choose a selection that contains both prints and solids. My maximalist taste usually leads me to choose a large variety of prints for a bold look. For a cleaner, more minimalist look, try choosing all solids. A combination of prints and solids will help create balance.

SHOP FOR PRECUTS

Precuts are a great way to take the guesswork out of fabric selection. Most precut bundles include 1 piece of each print in a fabric collection. These fabrics were designed to coordinate with one another. Choosing yardage from the same collection or designer will virtually eliminate any other guesswork.

ALTERNATE COLOR SCHEMES

Many of the projects in this book feature alternate versions. This was a deliberate decision so that you'd have a vision of what these projects would look like in a different color scheme.

Linen

Quilter's linen is my go-to basic for many projects. Different from traditional linen fabrics that have a tendency to heavily wrinkle and shrink, modern quilter's linens are a sturdy cotton/linen blend. They add gorgeous texture to any project. My personal favorite is Essex Yarn Dyed linens from Robert Kaufman Fabrics, which are a 55% cotton / 45% linen blend. Another favorite is Mochi Linen from Moda Fabrics + Supplies, which comes in both solids and dots. They are a blend of unbleached 70% cotton / 30% linen, and are a little bit sturdier than Essex linen, which makes them ideal for bags and home decor projects.

Wool

Wool is an excellent choice for raw edge appliqué projects because its edges don't easily fray. There are many excellent hand-dyed, felted wools for quilting. While pricey, the texture and dimension that wool adds to a project make it well worth the cost. Many shops that offer hand-dyed wool have scrap bags and bundles that are great stash builders. Even the tiniest scraps can be used in appliqué projects.

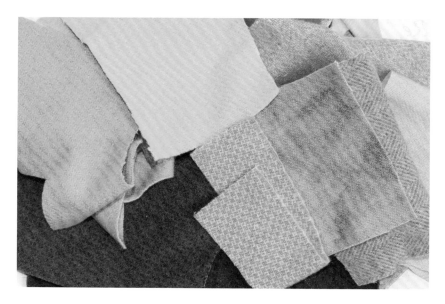

Wool–Blend Felt

A recent favorite for appliqué is wool-blend felt. Different from *felted wool*, wool-blend felt is a nonwoven wool/rayon blend. Unlike craft felt, which is 100% man-made materials, wool-blend felt can withstand the heat of an iron to be used for fusible appliqué. It still is loftier than cotton and linen, which creates texture and dimension in your appliqué projects, but at a much lower price tag than 100% hand-dyed felted wool.

For use in quilting projects, first machine wash wool-blend felt with a mild detergent and a color catcher to absorb excess dye. Tumble dry with medium heat. Press with a hot, dry iron. If necessary, use a peel-and-stick lint roller to remove any fuzz from the surface. Then appliqué as you would felted wool.

This has become my go-to for larger appliqué motifs, as it's significantly reduced the cost of making wool appliqué projects. I use a combination of 100% felted wool and wool-blend felt in all the appliqué projects throughout this book. The combination works well together and adds amazing texture.

Repurposing Clothing

Another option is to repurpose clothing. The denim used in the Purr-fect Pocket Tote (page 50) was repurposed from a beloved pair of jeans that had torn. If you don't have a pair of your own jeans you're ready to part with, visit a local thrift shop and you'll be sure to find something that will work for your projects. Just make sure the repurposed clothing is clean and dry before use.

Repurposed clothing is also a great way to find high-quality wool at a fraction of the cost. Search your local thrift and consignment shops. You'd be surprised what you can find. Wool sweaters, suits, and other apparel are often made with high-quality wool. Just because it's no longer fashionable to wear as clothing doesn't mean it won't work for your appliqué project!

To felt wool from thrifted apparel, simply machine wash with a mild detergent, then tumble dry with high heat. The result will be felted wool, ready for appliqué.

Repurposed denim on the Purr-fect Pocket Tote (page 50)

Vinyl

A few of the projects in this book call for clear vinyl. It may seem intimidating, but don't worry. Looks can be deceiving. For these projects, choose a heavy-weight vinyl, in the 12-gauge to 16-gauge range. C&T Publishing carries an excellent product called Premium Clear Vinyl. This 12-gauge vinyl can be purchased on their website (ctpub.com). You can also purchase clear vinyl by the yard in a variety of gauges at many sewing and craft retailers.

TIPS FOR WORKING WITH VINYL

- *Use an adhesive tape, such as Tear-Perfect Maker Tape by Judy Gauthier (from C&T Publishing) or Wonder Tape, to secure edges for sewing. Pinholes won't heal in vinyl. If attaching binding, use Wonder Clips to hold the binding material.*

- *Purchase more than required. If you make a mistake and have to take out a seam, the holes won't go away. Fortunately, vinyl is very affordable.*

- *A walking foot or Teflon foot will make it easier to feed the layers evenly through your machine's feed dogs.*

- *A heavy-gauge needle, such as an upholstery or leather needle, and polyester thread will make stitching through vinyl easier.*

Adding Embellishments to Your Projects

Adding embellishments to your projects—whether it's to a quilt or a bag—is a great way to add texture and give your project a little something extra.

Embellishing your quilts with some hand embroidery or decorative stitches is a fabulous extra touch. Go ahead! Add a little bit of bling to your zipper pouch with a leather tassel or a decorative charm. Don't be afraid to experiment with embellishments to find out what suits your taste.

Added details on the Hiss and Make Up Bag (page 37)

Quilting

Quilting is an obvious way to add texture. The method of quilting is dependent on individual tastes and specific projects. Dense, custom machine quilting may not be appropriate for every project. Sometimes, you want the focus to be on the beautiful patchwork, so a simple quilting design will do. Other times, you may want to create texture and emphasis in negative spaces. And some projects may call for more whimsical big-stitch hand quilting. However you approach it, quilting your projects is sure to create some lovely texture.

Quilting detail on *Feline Floral* quilt (page 108). Custom quilting by Charisma Horton.

Making the Back of Your Quilt as Pretty as the Front

You've spent countless hours making sure your quilt top is absolutely purr-fect. So why stop with the front of your quilt? I've long subscribed to the notion that the back of my quilts should look as pretty as the front. Something to which you've devoted so much time and effort deserves to look gorgeous from every angle.

Backing Your Quilt

There are some projects in this book where I've based my color scheme for a quilt entirely on a large-scale fabric print that I loved too much to cut up! So instead of cutting up that print to use in patchwork, I've used the yardage as the backing for my quilt. It's like having a second quilt to love! One side is the patchwork and appliqué I've worked so hard to make purr-fect. And the other side is like a wholecloth quilt I get to admire every time I use my quilt.

TIP **Short on Backing Fabric?** *Piecing leftover blocks or scraps into your backing fabric is another great way to make the back of your quilt as pretty as the front.*

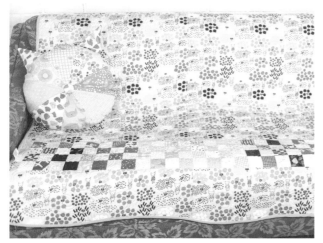

Detail of pieced back from *Chasing Dreams* (page 132)

Beautiful backings from *Purr-fect Patchwork* projects

Labeling Your Quilt

You made this thing of beauty—now own it! I label every quilt I make. From the time I started quilting, I was told that my quilts held no value until they were labeled. Whether or not this is actually true, I don't know. But artists sign their work. And I consider my quilts to be my art, so I sign them. There are a variety of ways to label your quilts. Let's take a look at a few that I like to use!

HAND-EMBROIDERED LABELS

A hand-embroidered label can be as simple as a piece of fabric hand embroidered with your initials and the year it was completed, or it can include your full name and the details of your quilt. These pieces are then pieced into the backing fabric prior to quilting, or whipstitched to the back of your completed quilt.

Hand embroidered label detail on *Feline Floral* (page 108)

MACHINE EMBROIDERED LABELS

Nowadays, it's not uncommon to own an embroidery machine. Many domestic sewing machines even include an embroidery module. For several quilts included in this book, I used my embroidery machine to create custom labels that coordinated with the specific quilt. My favorite is this cat-food can label designed by the inimitable Tula Pink.

Label detail on *Blooming Curiosity* (page 102)

PREPRINTED LABELS

There are several options for preprinted labels. Some fabric designers have started creating quilt labels that are available as fabric panels. You can purchase them by the yard or by the panel from the bolt. You then have the option to fill in the pertinent information using a permanent, fine-tipped pen. Another option is iron-on labels. *Best-Ever Iron-On Quilt Labels* (by C&T Publishing) has over 100 preprinted iron-on labels. Just choose a label that's fitting for your project and iron the selected design onto fabric. If desired, labels can then be painted, embroidered, or colored to suit your needs. This flexible option allows for as much or as little effort as you wish to contribute!

Label detail on *Ziggy Kitty* (page 120)

COMMERCIALLY PURCHASED LABELS

With the large number of quilts I make, it has become tedious to create something custom for each and every quilt. There are many businesses devoted entirely to creating labels. They come in a variety of materials—everything from stamped leather to printed twill to woven jacquard. Typically they are made in batches no smaller than 50 and are quite affordable. I purchased mine from Custom Labels 4 U (customlabels4u.com) and have been extremely pleased with the quality. They even offer metallic thread that fits my maximalist style. I simply stitch my labels into my quilt binding!

Front and back details from my custom, commercially made labels

PROJECTS

Here are a few tips to help get this party started:

• Read all instructions through completely before beginning.

• All seams are ¼″ unless otherwise noted.

• Fabrics are 44″/45″ wide unless otherwise noted. Usable width of fabric may vary.

• Due to differences among manufacturers, there may be a slight variation in the size of precuts. A fat quarter is a precut piece of fabric that measures 18″ × 20″–22″. A fat eighth is a precut piece of fabric that measures 9″ × 20″–22″. For projects that require precut squares, please measure beforehand to ensure that the squares are a full 5″ × 5″ or 10″ × 10″.

$\mathcal{H}$iss and Make Up Bag

FINISHED BAG: 4½″ × 8½″

The Hiss and Make Up Bag is a quick and easy project that is very versatile. In addition to being a makeup bag, it can also be used as a pencil bag or a pouch for carrying your hand stitching. This easy-to-make bag is a great gift for your cat-loving friends!

MATERIALS

QUILTER'S LINEN: 1 fat quarter for bag exterior, ears, and binding

CAT-THEMED COTTON PRINT: 1 fat eighth for bag interior

HEAVY-GAUGE TRANSPARENT VINYL: ¼ yard for bag back

WOOL-BLEND FELT: Small scraps for eyes and nose

BATTING: ¼ yard of fusible fleece

FUSIBLE FOAM INTERFACING: ⅛ yard (I like Pellon's FF78F1 Flex-Foam 1-Sided Fusible.)

PAPER-BACKED FUSIBLE WEB: Small scrap

PERLE COTTON: Size 8 for whiskers

METAL COIL ZIPPER: 7″

ZIPPER FOOT

TEMPLATE PLASTIC

WONDER CLIPS

Optional Materials

WONDER TAPE: ¼″

METAL SPLIT RING: ¼″

SUEDE TASSEL: ¾″–1″

Cutting

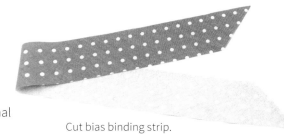

Cut bias binding strip.

Template plastic

• Trace and cut the ear pattern (page 43).

Quilter's linen

• Fold the fat quarter diagonally and finger-press to create a diagonal crease. Cut on the crease; then cut 1 strip 2½″ wide. Set aside.

• From the remainder, cut 1 rectangle 4½″ × 8½″, 1 rectangle 2″ × 8½″, and 1 square 3″ × 3″. Cut 4 using the ear pattern.

Cat-themed cotton print, heavy-gauge transparent vinyl, and fusible fleece

• Cut 1 rectangle 4½″ × 8½″ from *each*.

Wool-blend felt

• Trace the eye and nose patterns (page 43) on paper-backed fusible web. Fuse to the wool-blend felt; then cut the shapes.

Fusible foam interfacing

• Cut 2 using the ear pattern.

Construction

Make the Ears

1 Fuse a foam interfacing ear piece to a fabric ear piece following the manufacturer's instructions. Repeat with another ear piece from each.

2 Place the remaining fabric ear pieces on top of the fused pieces, right sides together. Sew with a ¼″ seam allowance around the outside edges, leaving the bottom edge of the pieces *open*.

3 Trim the points, being careful not to clip too close to the stitching (see Just a Little Off the Top, page 25).

4 Turn the ears right side out through the bottom. Press. Topstitch a scant ¼″ around the outside of the pieces.

Make the Face

1 Transfer the whisker design (page 43) to the linen rectangle 4½″ × 8½″ using your preferred method. For this project, I recommend a light source and a heat- or water-erasable transfer pen. The center of each set of whiskers should be about 2¼″ from the top edge and ¾″ from the outside edges.

2 Hand embroider the whiskers using a running stitch (page 17) and size 8 perle cotton.

3 Fuse the embroidered rectangle to the matching rectangle of fusible fleece following manufacturer's instructions.

4 Fold the piece in half vertically and finger-press to mark the center. Fuse the nose piece on the center crease 2¼″ from the top edge. Fuse the eye pieces 1″ on either side of the nose, aligning the bottom of each eye with the top of the nose.

5 Topstitch the eyes and nose with a coordinating color of thread.

Prepare the Zipper

1 Fold the linen square 3″ × 3″ in half and press. Unfold; then press the raw edges inward to meet the crease. Press in half again.

2 Cut in half to create 2 zipper-tape ends ¾″ × 1½″.

3 Place the ends of the zipper tape inside the fold of the fabric. Trim the edges to the width of the zipper tape. Topstitch close to the inner fold of the fabric. **A**

A

Note Measure the length of the zipper tape before beginning. The 7″ zipper I used had an 8½″ zipper tape. If necessary, change the dimensions of the zipper-tape ends to fit your zipper tape. Stitching over metal zipper teeth can cause broken needles or damage your machine!

Make the Vinyl Piece Binding

1 Press the linen rectangle 2″ × 8½″ in half lengthwise. Unfold and press the raw edges inward toward the crease. Press in half again.

2 Insert a long edge of the vinyl rectangle into the binding strip. Hold in place with tape or glue. **B**

B

Assemble the Bag

1 Position each ear piece 1½″ in from the outer edge along the top edge of the face unit, right sides together. Baste in place a scant ⅛″ from the raw edges. **C**

2 With right sides together, align the top edge of the face unit with the edge of zipper tape. The zipper pull should be on the right. Place the cat print rectangle right side down, aligning the top edge with the zipper-tape edge. Pin or clip the layers together. Using a zipper foot, sew a ¼″ seam along the pinned edge. Backstitch at the beginning and end of the seam. **D**

3 Fold the wrong sides together, pressing away from the zipper tape and making sure that ears are now pointed up. Topstitch through all 3 layers, close to the previous seam. **E**

4 With the zipper facing up, clip or tape the bound vinyl piece to the edge of the zipper tape. Sew the vinyl piece to the zipper tape, stitching close to both folds of the binding. **F**

5 Fold the bag in half so that the zipper is at the top. Hold the layers together using clips. Using your favorite marking tool, trace the rim of a disposable plastic cup aligned with the bottom corners of the bag. Trim the fabric to create the bag's rounded corners. **G**

6 If necessary, trim any excess vinyl from the edges.

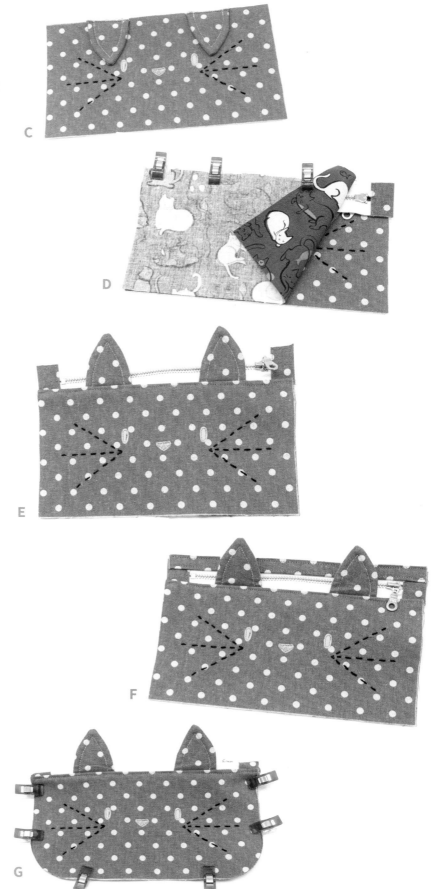

C

D

E

F

G

Finishing

1 Square the ends of the set aside bias binding strip. Press under ½″ on one short end. Then press the binding strip in half lengthwise, wrong sides together. **H**

2 Beginning with the turned end of the binding strip, secure the raw edges of the strip to the raw edges of the *vinyl* side of the bag using clips. **I**

3 Stop placing the clips once you've gone around the second rounded corner. Trim the strip about ½″ past the bag's edge. Fold under the ½″ excess and *carefully* press the end, making sure not to touch the vinyl with the iron. Continue placing the clips for the rest of the edges. Machine stitch in place using a ¼″ seam allowance. Backstitch at both ends. **J**

4 Fold the binding to the front of the bag. Finish by hand, as you would traditional quilt binding. **K**

5 If using, attach your tassel (or charm, or other fun embellishment) to your zipper pull with a split ring in a coordinating finish.

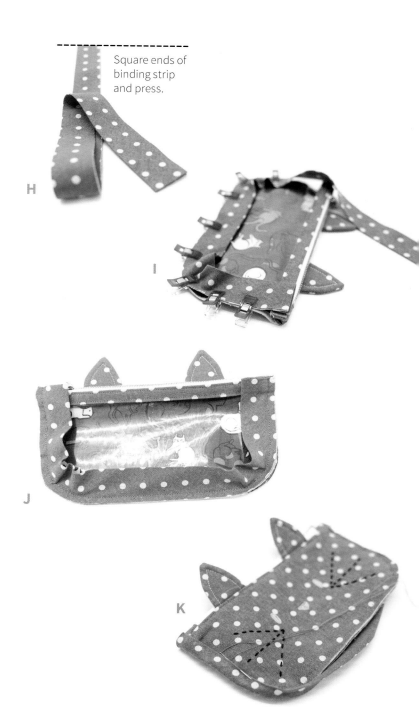

Square ends of binding strip and press.

H

I

J

K

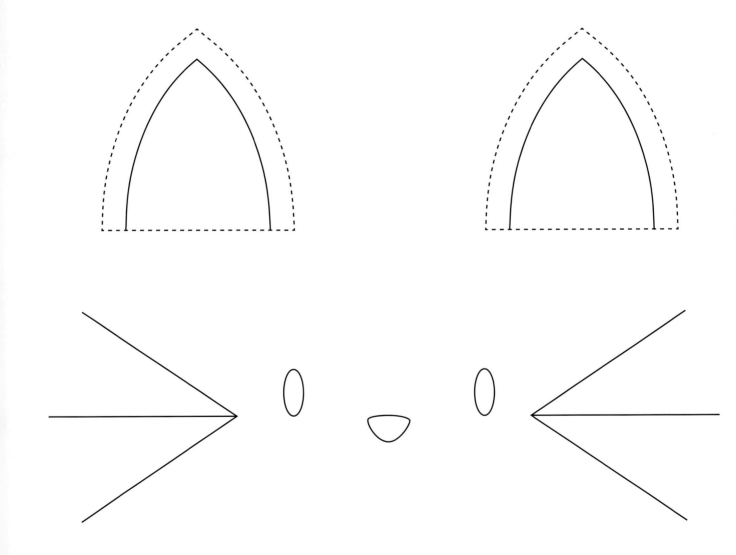

Tuxedo Cat Wristlet

FINISHED BAG: 6″ × 6″, excluding strap

The Tuxedo Cat Wristlet is perfect for the cat lover on the go! Small and portable, this bag has just enough room for the essentials but is packed with style.

MATERIALS

ASSORTED BLACK PRINTS: ⅓ yard total for bag front

BLACK PRINT 1: 1 fat quarter for bag interior and wrist strap

BLACK PRINT 2: 1 fat eighth for bag back

BLACK SOLID: ⅛ yard for binding

FUSIBLE FLEECE: ¼ yard

FUSIBLE FOAM INTERFACING: ⅛ yard
(I like Pellon's FF78F1 Flex-Foam 1-Sided Fusible.)

ZIPPER: 6″

ZIPPER FOOT

SWIVEL CLASP AND D-RING: ⅝″

WONDER CLIPS

Cutting

Template plastic

- Trace and cut the ear pattern (page 49).

Assorted black prints

- Cut a total of 7 squares 2½″ × 2½″.
- Cut 2 squares 2¾″ × 2¾″; subcut in half diagonally.
- Cut 4 squares 3″ × 3″; cut 2 and 2 reversed using the ear pattern.

Black print 1

- Cut 1 strip 6½″ × width of fat quarter; subcut into 1 rectangle 2½″ × 6½″, 1 rectangle 4½″ × 6½″, and 1 square 6½″ × 6½″.
- Cut 1 strip 2″ × 18″.
- Cut 1 square 2″ × 2″.

Black print 2

- Cut 1 square 6½″ × 6½″.

Fusible fleece

- Cut 1 strip 6½″ × width of fabric; subcut into 1 rectangle 2½″ × 6½″, 1 rectangle 4½″ × 6½″, and 1 square 6½″ × 6½″.

Black solid

- Cut 1 strip 2¼″ × width of fabric.

Construction

Make the Ears

1 Fuse a foam interfacing ear piece to a fabric ear piece following manufacturer's instructions. Repeat with a reversed ear piece from each.

2 Place the remaining fabric ear pieces on top of the fused pieces, right sides together. Sew with a ¼″ seam allowance around the outside edges, leaving the bottom edge of the pieces *open*.

3 Trim the points, being careful not to clip too close to the stitching (see Just a Little Off the Top, page 25).

4 Turn the ears right side out through the bottom. Press. Topstitch ¼″ around the outside of the pieces.

Make the Bag Front

1 Sew together 3 assorted black print squares 2½″ × 2½″ in a row. Press the seams open. Following the manufacturer's instructions, fuse the pieced row to a fusible fleece rectangle 2½″ × 6½″. If desired, hand or machine quilt the section. Set aside. **A**

2 Sew together another 3 assorted black print squares 2½″ × 2½″ in a row. Press the seams open.

A

3 Sew 2 half-square triangles 2¾″ × 2¾″ to the sides of the remaining assorted black print square 2½″ × 2½″. Press the seams open.

4 Sew the rows from Steps 2 and 3 together, matching the seams. Press the seam open. **B**

5 Following the manufacturer's instructions, fuse the joined rows to the fusible fleece rectangle 4½″ × 6½″. Trim the excess fleece from the bottom corners. If desired, hand or machine quilt the section.

B

Prepare the Zipper

1 Move the zipper pull to the center of the zipper. Trim the zipper to exactly 6½″, making sure to trim from *both* ends of the zipper tape.

2 Hand stitch a scant ⅛″ from the cut ends, using a short, straight stitch. Backstitch over each end several times. This will prevent your zipper pull from sliding off while constructing the rest of the bag. **C**

C

D

E

F

Attach the Zipper

1 With right sides facing up, place the zipper on top of a black print 1 rectangle 2½″ × 6½″, aligning the top edges. Then layer the set-aside fused bag front panel right side down, aligning the bottom edge of the panel with the top edge of the zipper. Using clips to hold them in place, sew the layers together using a zipper foot. Backstitch at the beginning and end of the seam. **D**

2 Press the layers away from the zipper tape. Topstitch close to the previous seam. **E**

3 With right sides facing up, place the zipper unit on top of a black print 1 rectangle 4½″ × 6½″, aligning the top edges. Layer the remaining fused bag front panel, wrong side up, aligning the top edge of the panel with the edge of the zipper. Using clips to hold them in place, sew the layers together using a zipper foot. Backstitch at the beginning and end of the seam. **F**

4 Press the layers away from the zipper tape. Topstitch close to the previous seam. Trim the excess interior fabric from the bottom corners. **G**

G

Attach the Ears

Measure ⅜″ in from either side of the bag front and make a small mark on the top edge. Align the raw edges of each ear piece with the top edge of the bag, positioning the outer straight edge of the pieces at the ⅜″ marks. Baste in place. **H**

H

Make the D-Ring Tab

1 Press the black print 1 square 2″ × 2″ in half. Unfold; then press the raw edges inward to meet the crease. Press in half again to make a ½″ × 2″ folded piece. Topstitch a scant ⅛″ from the folded edges. **I**

I

2 Slip the tab through the D-ring. Fold in half so that the raw edges meet. Align the tab with the right edge of the bag front, approximately ¾″ from the top edge. Baste in place, taking care not to catch the ear piece in the stitching. **J**

J

Make the Bag Back

1 Fuse the fusible fleece square 6½″ × 6½″ to the black print 2 square 6½″ × 6½″. Sandwich with the black print 1 square 6½″ × 6½″. Quilt as desired.

2 Align the fused and/or quilted back with the bag front, wrong sides together. Trim the back's bottom corners to match the bag front. **K**

K

Construct the Bag

1 Unzip the zipper at least halfway. Pin the bag back to the bag front, right sides together. Sew around the edges with a ¼″ seam allowance, pivoting carefully at the corners. Backstitch at the beginning and end. **L**

2 Turn the bag right side out through the open zipper to make sure the ears are not caught in the seams. Then turn the bag wrong side out again, leaving the zipper open.

L

Bind the Bag

1 Press the black solid strip 2¼″ × width of fabric in half to form a binding strip.

2 Starting at the top edge of the bag, align the raw edges of the binding with the raw edges of the bag and sew, leaving about a 1″ tail unsewn at the beginning.

3 Stop approximately ¼″ from each corner. Fold the binding away from the seam to match the angle of the bag corner; then fold back down again in line with the bag edge. Continue stitching in this manner until you're about 2½″ from your starting point.

4 Trim the remaining binding strip approximately 1½″ past the starting point. Fold and press under about ½″ of fabric. Insert the 1″ tail of fabric into the folded end of the binding. Continue stitching as before, backstitching when you reach the end of the binding. **M**

M

5 Wrap the binding over to the other side of the seam. Using a blind stitch, secure folded edge of binding in place, taking care to fold and secure the miters. **N**

N

Finishing

1 Turn the bag right side out through the open zipper. Press.

2 Press the black print 1 strip 2″ × 18″ in half lengthwise. Unfold; then press the raw edges inward to meet the crease. Fold in half again to form ½″ × 18″ strap. Topstitch close to both folded edges. **O**

3 Fold the strap in half and slide through the closed end of the swivel clasp. Join the ends by stitching a scant ⅛″ from the raw ends. **P**

4 Turn the strap so that the sewn ends now face inward. Move the swivel clasp down to the seam. Carefully topstitch across the strap as close to the clasp as possible. Topstitch again approximately ¼″ from the previous stitching. **Q**

TIP *Using a zipper foot when topstitching will help you get closer to the bag hardware without breaking your needle or damaging your machine!*

5 Using the swivel clasp, attach the finished strap to the D-ring. And just like that, you're ready to go!

O

P

Q

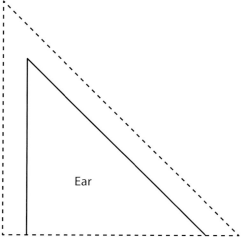

Ear

$\mathcal{P}$urr-fect Pocket Tote

FINISHED BAG: 13″ × 13″ × 5″, excluding straps

This project began as a way to upcycle a favorite pair of jeans that had torn irreparably. Does it get more purr-fect *than a kitty peeking out of a pocket? I think not. Both functional and adorable, this tote is a great way to enjoy those jeans for a few more years* and *show off your cat-lady status all at the same time!*

MATERIALS

LOW-VOLUME PRINT: ½ yard for bag exterior

MAGENTA PRINT 1: ½ yard for bag interior

MAGENTA PRINT 2: 1 fat quarter for interior zipper pocket

MAGENTA PRINT 3: 1½ yards for straps

MAGENTA WOOL-BLEND FELT: 6″ × 9″ piece for cat

LIME GREEN WOOL: 2″ × 2 scrap for ears and flower centers

TURQUOISE WOOL: 4″ × 4 scrap for flowers

Polypropylene webbing: 3 yards, 1″ wide for straps

LIGHTWEIGHT WOVEN FUSIBLE INTERFACING: 1 yard (I like Pellon's SF101 Shape-Flex.)

BAG STABILIZER: 18″ × 58″ package of ByAnnie's Soft and Stable

PAPER-BACKED FUSIBLE WEB: ⅛ yard

6-STRAND EMBROIDERY FLOSS: Lime green

NYLON COIL ZIPPER: 9″ or longer

MAGNETIC SNAP SET: ¾″

JEANS: 1 old pair (Jeans with a back pocket no larger than 6½″ square is ideal.)

MARKING PEN, such as FriXion (by Pilot)

ZIPPER FOOT

ELMER'S GLUE OR MAKER'S TAPE

Cutting

Low-volume print

- Cut 2 rectangles 11½″ × 15″.

Magenta print 1

- Cut 2 rectangles 14½″ × 16½″.

Magenta print 2

- Cut 1 rectangle 9″ × 18″.

Magenta print 3

- Cut 2 strips 4″ × 51″ from the *length of fabric*.

Appliqué motifs

- Trace the appliqué patterns (page 59) onto paper-backed fusible web.
- Fuse and cut 1 cat motif from the magenta wool-blend felt.
- Fuse and cut 2 inner ears and 3 flower centers from the lime green wool.
- Fuse and cut 3 flowers from the turquoise wool.

Polypropylene webbing

- Cut 2 strips each 51″ long.

Bag stabilizer

- Cut 2 rectangles 15″ × 17″.

Lightweight woven fusible interfacing

- Cut 2 rectangles 14½″ × 16½″.

Jeans

- Carefully remove one back pocket using a seam ripper. Alternatively, you can cut the back pocket from the jeans and then cut away the excess fabric from the inside, trimming as close to the pocket seams as possible.
- Cut the jeans apart at the inner leg seams. From the widest part of the legs, cut 2 rectangles 6½″ × 15.″

Construction

Exterior Construction

1 Layer each low-volume print rectangle right side up on a rectangle of Soft and Stable, aligning the top 15″ edges. Quilt as desired, quilting the fabric portion *only*. **A**

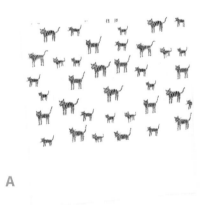

A

Note Soft and Stable will shrink approximately ½″ when quilted. This is to be expected and has been allowed for in the cutting instructions.

---

2 Choose one of the quilted pieces for the bag front. Find the center of the front piece and the jeans pocket by folding each in half vertically and finger-pressing. Align the crease in the pocket with the crease in the bag front. Place the pocket so the bottom is 10½″ from the top of the bag front. Trace the pocket to mark the placement using an erasable marking tool, such as a FriXion pen. **B**

B

Appliqué the Bag Front

1 Transfer the cat face onto the felt appliqué piece. Embroider the face using a backstitch and 3 strands of lime green floss. Position the green inner-ear motifs on top of the cat. Fuse in place; then machine or hand appliqué using the desired stitch.

2 Position the felt cat on the bag front so the bottom will be about ¾″ inside the pocket. Fuse and appliqué in place using the method of your choosing. Arrange the flowers so that they're floating just above the pocket placement. Fuse and stitch in place. **C**

Attach the Exterior Pocket

Pin the pocket in position and machine stitch around the outside of the pocket, following the original stitching and leaving the top edge open. If there are 2 rows of stitching on the outer edges of your pocket, follow both rows of stitching. Backstitch at the beginning and end of the stitching. **D**

Strap Construction

1 Press both magenta print 3 strips in half lengthwise. Unfold; then press the raw edges inward to meet the crease. **E**

2 Open the strips and insert a 51″ strip of poly webbing in each. **F**

TIP *Use a cigarette lighter to melt the ends of the poly webbing to prevent unraveling!*

3 Fold the fabric back over the webbing. Press the entire strap in half again. Topstitch a scant ⅛″ from both folded edges of each strap. **G**

C

Appliqué and embroidery placement

D

E

F

G

Strap Placement

1 Measure 6″ from the bottom edge of the bag exterior pieces and mark a horizontal line. This will be the placement for the bottom of the denim pocket. Measure 2½″ in from each side. Draw a vertical line from the denim placement line to the top of the bag exterior to mark the strap placement lines. **H**

2 Fold each strap in half lengthwise. Mark the centers with pins. Measuring from the raw ends, draw horizontal lines 9¾″ and 10½″ from both ends of each strap. **I**

3 Starting about 1″ below the marked denim placement line, pin the straps to both the front and back exterior pieces, aligning the outside edge of the straps with the strap placement lines. Check to be sure that handles are the same length while pinned. If they appear uneven, make adjustments and re-pin.

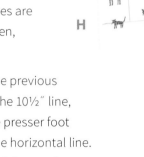

H

I

4 Stitch each strap to the bag pieces following the previous topstitching. Stop stitching when you've reached the 10½″ line, and, with your needle in the down position, lift the presser foot and carefully turn the bag so that you can stitch the horizontal line. Stitch across the line and stop once you've reached the previous topstitching. Again, with the needle in the down position, pivot the bag and continue sewing until you've reached the raw end of the strap. **J**

5 To reinforce the straps, also stitch across the 9¾″ line, stopping at the topstitching and pivoting at each corner until you've stitched a square. Then sew an X through the square. **K**

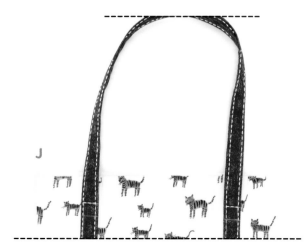

J

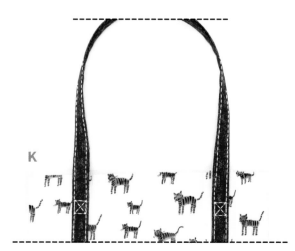

K

L

M

N

Finish the Exterior

1 Place the denim rectangles on top of the bag exterior pieces, aligning the 15″ edge with the marked placement line. Stitch using a ¼″ seam allowance. **L**

2 Open and press each denim piece so that it covers the exposed Soft and Stable stabilizer. Topstitch close to the seam.

3 Baste the outer edges of the denim pieces; then quilt as desired. Each quilted exterior panel should measure 14½″ × 16½.″ Trim to size if needed. **M**

4 Cut a square 3″ × 3″ from the bottom corners of both bag exterior panels. **N**

5 Fold the cut edges of the corner to meet one another. Pin together. Sew the cut edges using a ¼″ seam allowance. Backstitch at the beginning and end. Press. Repeat with the remaining corners. **O**

6 Turn an exterior panel inside out. Pin the straps to the center to avoid catching in the seams. Nest the other exterior panel inside of the other, with right sides together. Using a ⅜″ seam allowance, stitch the outside edges, leaving the top of the bag *open*. **P**

7 Turn the bag exterior right side out, gently pressing the bottom corners outward. Leave the straps pinned out of the way for now.

Prepare the Interior

1 Fuse the interfacing rectangles to the wrong side of each magenta print 1 rectangle.

2 Cut squares 3″ × 3″ from the bottom corners of both interior pieces. **Q**

O

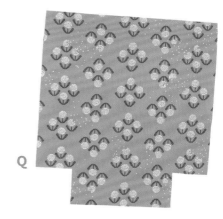

P

Q

Attach the Magnetic Snaps

1 Finger-press the interior panels in half lengthwise to mark center. Remove the washers from the back side of the snaps. Position the washers on the wrong side of the interior panels, aligned with the center crease and 1½˝ from the top edge.

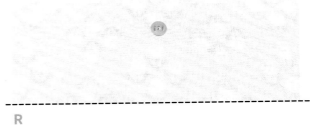

2 Using the washers as a guide, mark the prong position on both panels. With a seam ripper, carefully cut a small slit at each mark. **R**

R

3 Slide the prongs through the slits from the right side of the fabric. Place the prongs through the washer. Fold the prongs outward, flat against the washer, to secure. Repeat with the remaining snap on the other panel. **S**

S

Make the Interior Zipper Pocket

1 Choose one of the interior panels for the zipper pocket.

2 Place the magenta print 2 rectangle wrong side up, with a 9˝ edge at the top. Mark the zipper placement by measuring and marking a horizontal line 9½˝ from the top. Draw a second line ½˝ below the first. **T**

> **TIP** *To avoid confusion down the road, it's helpful to make a small marking on the wrong side of the fabric at the top edge of the pocket piece.*

3 Measure 1˝ in from the sides of the pocket piece and draw a short vertical line between the horizontal lines. **U**

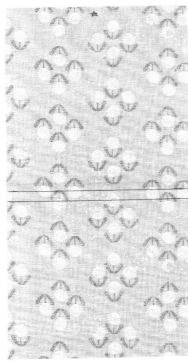

T

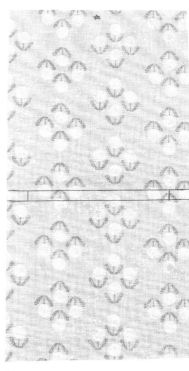

U

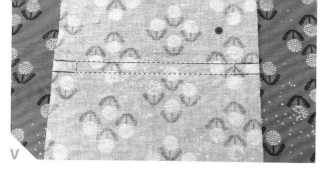

V

W

4 Finger-press both the interior panel and pocket piece in half vertically. Layer the pocket piece on the interior panel, right sides together, aligning the center creases and with the zipper markings 2″–2½″ below the magnetic snap. Pin in place.

5 Sew on the lines, creating a long rectangular box. **V**

6 Draw a horizontal line in the center of the rectangular box, stopping approximately ¼″ from each end. Draw a small inward-facing V at each end to meet the centerline. Using a seam ripper to start, cut along the lines through both layers of fabric with small, sharp scissors, taking care not to cut through the stitching. **W**

TIP *Cut as close to the stitching as you can without cutting into the stitching. This will help prevent puckering around the zipper.*

7 Turn the pocket piece to the wrong side of the interior panel through the cut opening. Press. **X**

8 With the interior panel right side up, center the zipper under the bag opening. To prevent a wavy zipper, baste in place with Elmer's Glue or Maker's Tape rather than pinning in place.

9 Make sure that the pocket piece is flat and away from the opening. Using a zipper foot, topstitch ⅛″ around the opening to secure the zipper in place. **Y**

10 Fold the pocket piece in half, matching the edges and corners. Sew the side and bottom edges, using a ¼″ seam allowance and taking care to keep the interior panel out of the way. **Z**

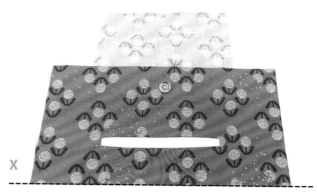

X

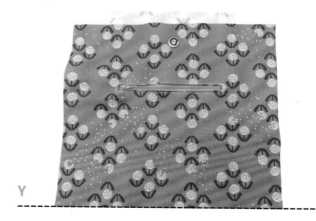

Y

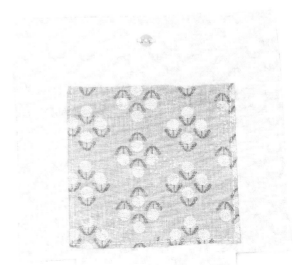

Z

Finishing the Interior

1 Fold the cut edges of each panel corner together and sew with a ¼˝ seam allowance in the same manner as the exterior panels. Press. **A**

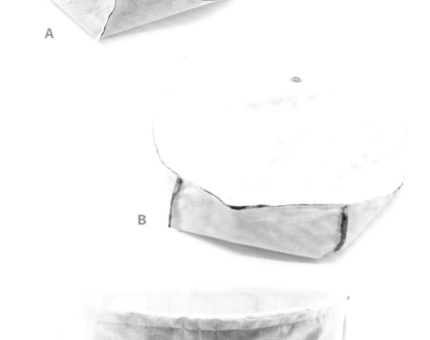

A

2 Turn one interior panel inside out. Nest the other interior panel inside of the other, with right sides together. Using a ⅜˝ seam allowance, stitch the outside edges, leaving a 6˝ opening in the bottom edge for turning. Leave the interior section wrong side out. **B**

B

Final Bag Assembly

1 With the straps still pinned to the center of the bag exterior, nest the bag exterior inside of the bag interior, right sides together. Align the top edges and stitch using a ½˝ seam allowance. **C**

TIP *It may be necessary to use a heavier-gauge needle, such as a denim or upholstery needle, when stitching through such thick layers of fabric!*

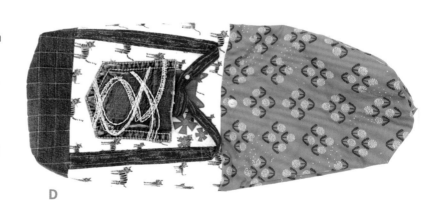

C

2 Turn the bag right side out through the opening in the bag interior. Hand or machine stitch the opening closed. **D**

3 Gently tuck the interior inside the bag. Press. With the straps still pinned out of the way, topstitch ⅛˝ around the top edge of the bag. **E**

D

4 Unpin the straps and you're ready to use your Purr-fect Pocket Tote!

E

Tale of Two Kitties Needle Book

FINISHED NEEDLE BOOK: 5″ × 7″ closed, 10″ × 7″ open

Sometimes it's good to get out and get a little fresh air. But that doesn't mean you can't bring your sewing along with you! This "pawsitively" adorable needle book has plenty of room for all of your hand-stitching essentials but is compact enough to take just about anywhere. Just grab and go! Or dare I say, grab and sew?

MATERIALS

LOW-VOLUME PRINT 1: 1 fat quarter for book exterior

LOW-VOLUME PRINT 2: 1 fat eighth for book interior

DARK GREEN PRINT 1: 1 fat eighth for book exterior

DARK GREEN PRINT 2: 1 fat eighth or ⅛ yard for exterior cats

LIGHT GREEN PRINT 1: 1 fat eighth for zippered pouch

LIGHT GREEN PRINT 2: 1 fat eighth for divided pocket

SMALL SOLID SCRAPS: A variety for Flying Geese

GREEN WOOL-BLEND FELT: 6″ × 9″ piece for needle holder

HEAVY-GAUGE TRANSLUCENT VINYL: ⅛ yard for zipper pouch

FUSIBLE FLEECE: ¼ yard

LIGHTWEIGHT WOVEN INTERFACING: ¼ yard
(I like Pellon's SF101 Shape-Flex.)

NYLON-COIL ZIPPER: 7″

CORD ELASTIC for book closure

BUTTON: ¼″ for book closure

FOUNDATION PAPER OR LIGHTWEIGHT COPY PAPER

WONDER TAPE OR MAKER'S TAPE

ADD-A-QUARTER RULER

WONDER CLIPS

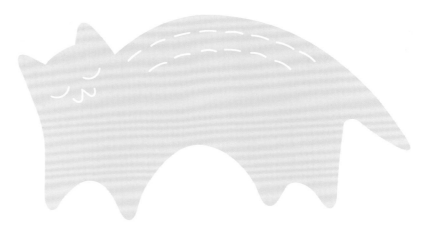

Cutting

Low-volume print 1
- Cut 2 rectangles 2¾″ × 3¼″.
- Cut 2 rectangles ¾″ × 3¼″.
- Cut 2 rectangles ¾″ × 3″.
- Cut 2 rectangles ¾″ × 5½″.
- Use the remainder for foundation paper piecing.

Low-volume print 2
- Cut 2 rectangles 5½″ × 7½″.

Dark green print 1
- Cut 1 rectangle 5½″ × 7½″.

Light green print 1
- Cut 1 square 5″ × 5″.
- Cut 2 rectangles 3¾″ × 7½″.
- Cut 2 rectangles 1¾″ × 7½″.

Light green print 2
- Cut 1 rectangle 5½″ × 8½″.

Green wool-blend felt
- Cut 1 rectangle 2½″ × 4″.

Heavy-gauge translucent vinyl
- Cut 1 rectangle 2½″ × 5″.

Fusible fleece
- Cut 1 rectangle 7½″ × 10½″.

Construction

Foundation Paper Piecing

1. Make 2 copies of each of the cat-head foundation patterns and 1 copy of the Flying Geese foundation pattern (page 67).

2. Referring to Foundation Paper Piecing Like a Purr-fessional (page 19), foundation paper piece 2 each of sections A and B and 1 Flying Geese section.

3. Remove the paper from the foundation paper-pieced units.

4. Join sections A and B to make 2 cat units. **A**

A

Assemble the Front Cover

Press all seams open.

1. Using low-volume print 1 pieces, sew 1 rectangle ¾″ × 3″ to the left edge of each cat unit. Sew 1 rectangle ¾″ × 3¼″ to the bottom edge of each cat unit.

2. Sew 1 rectangle 2¾″ × 3¼″ to the right edge of each cat unit. Sew 1 rectangle ¾″ × 5½″ to the top edge of each cat unit.

3. Arrange and sew the cat units to the Flying Geese unit, making sure to turn each cat unit to face the appropriate direction.

4. Sew the dark green print 1 rectangle to the left edge of the assembled cat head / Flying Geese unit. **B**

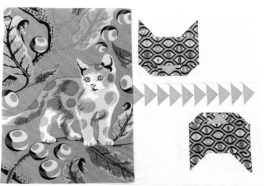

B

Finish the Cover

1 Following the manufacturer's instructions, fuse the fleece rectangle to the wrong side of the front cover. Quilt if desired. For this project, I chose to stitch-in-the-ditch.

2 Sew the button with sturdy thread in the center of the last Flying Geese triangle. **C**

3 Cut a piece of cord elastic about 3″ long. Fold in half. Place the elastic on the edge opposite the button, with the ends of the elastic overlapping the edge approximately ½″. Baste in place by stitching over the elastic a scant ⅛″ from the edge of the cover. **D**

Make the Zipper Pouch

1 Move the zipper pull to the center of the zipper. Trim the zipper tape to exactly 7½″, making sure to trim from both ends of the tape.

2 Press the light green print 1 square 5″ × 5″ in half. Unfold; then press the raw edges inward to meet the crease. Press in half again.

3 Cut in half to make 2 zipper-tape ends 1¼″ × 2½″ each. **E**

4 Insert the ends of the zipper tape into the zipper-tape ends. Stitch as close to the fold as possible. Trim the excess so that the edges are even with the zipper tape. **F**

5 Fuse lightweight interfacing to the wrong side of both light-green print 1 rectangles 3¾″ × 7½″.

6 On the wrong side of *each* interfaced rectangle 3¾″ × 7½″, draw a horizontal line 1″ from the top and bottom edges. Measure in 1½″ from each side and draw vertical lines. **G**

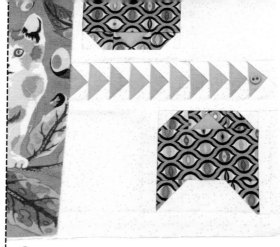

C

D

E

F

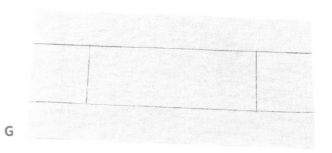

G

7 Draw an X through each box you just drew. Using a seam ripper to start, cut through each X with small, sharp scissors, stopping at the corners. **H**

8 Press under the edges to create a window. Trim each section of the X to a ¼″ seam allowance. **I**

9 Using Wonder Tape or a similar product, secure the vinyl to the wrong side of one of the window pieces to make the exterior zipper-pouch window.

10 Place the exterior window piece right side up. Place the zipper tape right side down along the top edge. Then layer the other window piece wrong side up, aligning the top edges. Using clips to hold them in place, sew the layers together with a ¼″ seam using a zipper foot. **J**

11 Carefully press away from the zipper tape. Avoid touching the iron to the vinyl. Using a zipper foot, topstitch close to the seam.

TIP *It is helpful to use a pressing cloth when ironing around vinyl. This will help you avoid melting the vinyl and making a sticky mess of your iron!*

12 Make sure the windows line up nicely; then topstitch close to the window through all the layers. Sew a second row of topstitching a scant ¼″ from the previous topstitching. **K**

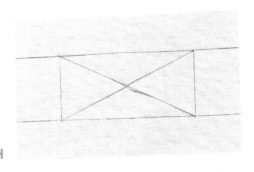

H

I

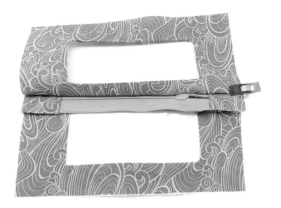

J

K

13 With right sides facing up, place the zipper section on top of 1 light-green print 1 rectangle 1¾″ × 7½″, aligning the raw edges. Layer another light-green print 1 rectangle 1¾″ × 7½″ wrong side up, aligning it with the zipper edge. Using clips to hold them in place, sew the layers together with a ¼″ seam using a zipper foot. **L**

L

14 Press the layers away from the zipper. Topstitch close to the seam. **M**

15 Fuse lightweight interfacing to the wrong side of *both* low-volume print 2 rectangles. Layer one of these pieces behind the zipper window section. Baste in place a scant ⅛″ around the edges. **N**

M

Note **Depending on the width of zipper tape used, you may need to trim the zipper pouch to 5½″ × 7½″. If so, make sure to trim evenly from each side so that the window remains centered.**

Make the Divided Pocket

1 Fuse lightweight interfacing to the wrong side of the light green print 2 rectangle. Press the rectangle in half, wrong sides together to form a 5½″ × 4¼″ rectangle. Topstitch close to the folded edge. **O**

N

2 Measuring from the left side of the pocket piece, draw a vertical line at 2¾″. Measure 1¼″ beyond that and draw a second vertical line. Layer the pocket on top of the right side of the remaining low-volume print 2 interfaced rectangle, aligning the raw edges of the pocket with the sides and bottom of the rectangle. Stitch on the drawn lines, backstitching at the top and bottom of the pocket. **P**

3 Baste the pocket to the rectangle by sewing a scant ⅛″ from the raw edges of the pocket.

O

P

Finish the Book Interior

1 Center the felt rectangle on the interfaced rectangle about ¼″ above the divided pocket. Pin in place to keep it from shifting. Topstitch in place, staying close to the felt edges. **Q**

2 Sew the pocket section to the zipper window section. Press the seam open. **R**

TIP *To help reduce bulk and make it easier to finish assembling the needle book, use a pair of small, sharp scissors to trim the interfacing from the seam allowances of the book's interior section.*

Finishing

1 Place the cover and the interior section right sides together. Sew around outer edges with ¼″ seam allowance, leaving a 3″–4″ opening for turning. **S**

2 Turn the needle book right side out through the opening. Press lightly, making sure that edges at the opening are pressed under. Topstitch around the entire exterior of the book, beginning at one Flying Geese seam and ending at the other to avoid the button. **T**

Q

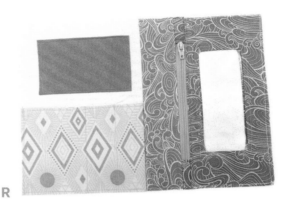

R

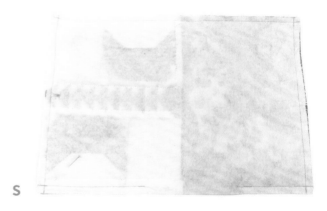

S

T

←Stop.

←Start.

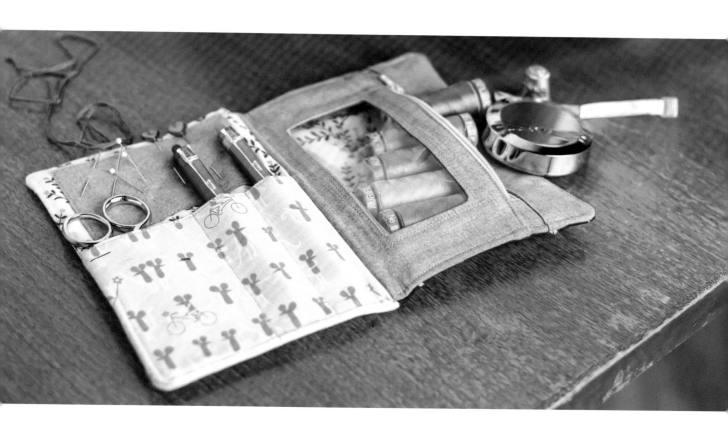

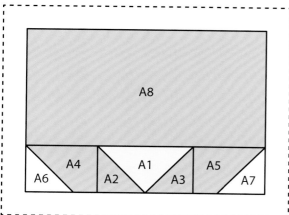

A8

A4 A1 A5
A6 A2 A3 A7

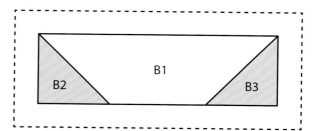

B1
B2 B3

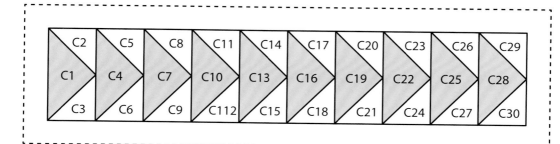

C2 C5 C8 C11 C14 C17 C20 C23 C26 C29
C1 C4 C7 C10 C13 C16 C19 C22 C25 C28
C3 C6 C9 C112 C15 C18 C21 C24 C27 C30

Stabby Tabby Pincushion

FINISHED PINCUSHION: 3″ wide × 6″ high × 3″ deep

Do you love "paw-ticipating" in quilting swaps? Or are you looking for a purr-fect gift for a quilty friend? Here's a great small gift that packs a lot of "paw-zazz." Fill the jar with some notions—or even better—a yummy treat to help boost your recipient's sewing mojo. No matter how you fill it, it's sure to be a hit with whomever receives it! Who knows? You might even love it so much you end up keeping it for yourself.

MATERIALS

GREEN PRINT SCRAPS: 8 squares 5″ × 5″ for pincushion

GREEN WOOL-BLEND FELT: 6″ × 9″ piece for ears and bottom of cushion

PINK WOOL-BLEND FELT: 1″ × 1″ scrap for nose

BUTTONS: 2, 3/8″ diameter for eyes

WIDE-MOUTH PINT-SIZE MASON JAR

RIBBON OR TWILL TAPE: ½ yard, ½″ wide

TEMPLATE PLASTIC

HOT GLUE GUN AND GLUE STICKS

CIGARETTE LIGHTER OR FRAY CHECK

GLUE STICK

HEAVY-DUTY POLYESTER THREAD

HAND SEWING NEEDLE

FIBERFILL (A higher-density fiberfill works best for this project.)

Cutting

Template plastic

- Trace and cut the wedge, base, ear, and nose patterns (page 71).

Green print scraps

- Cut 8 using the wedge pattern.

Green wool–blend felt

- Cut 1 using the base pattern and 2 using the ear pattern.

Pink wool–blend felt

- Cut 1 using the nose pattern.

Construction

Piece the Spokes

1 Align 2 wedge pieces along the long, straight edges, right sides together. Sew. Press the seam open. **A**

2 Continue piecing in this manner to make 2 half-circle units with 4 wedges each.

Add the Ears

1 Press each ear piece along the dotted line (shown on the pattern) with a hot, dry iron. Open. **B**

2 Align the bottom edges of the ear pieces with the straight edge of a half-circle unit. Position each ear so that the inner edge is ½″ from the center seam. Pin the ears in place to avoid shifting.

3 Sandwich the ears between the half-circle units, with the straight edges aligned and right sides together. Sew. Press the seam open. The ears should now be able to stand up on their own. **C**

Make the Face

1 Position the nose on the center seam, 1″ from the ears. Baste in position using a glue stick. Topstitch close to the edges of the nose piece.

2 Position each button eye in line with the top of the nose. When satisfied with the placement, hand sew in place with sturdy thread. **D**

Fill the Pincushion

1 Using a hand sewing needle and a length of heavy-duty polyester thread, sew a running stitch approximately ½″ from the edges of the pieced wedges. Leave 2 long thread tails when finished stitching. **E**

2 Pull the thread tails so that the piece forms a bowl or cup shape. Begin stuffing with fiberfill. The pincushion should be stuffed fairly full so that it

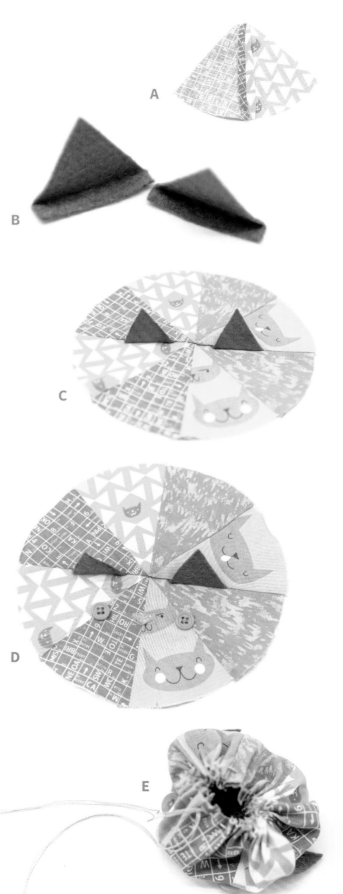

retains its shape but not so full that the outer ring of the mason jar won't fit over it. When the pincushion is sufficiently stuffed, pull the thread tails and knot. Trim the thread tails.

3 With needle and thread, whipstitch the felt base to cover the opening in the bottom of the pincushion. **F**

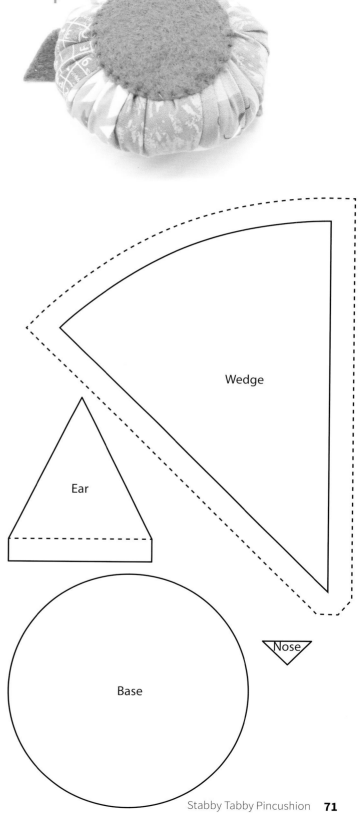

Attach the Cushion to the Jar

Separate the inner lid and outer ring from the jar. Apply a bead of hot glue to the felt base on the bottom of the pincushion; adhere it to the inner lid. Slide the outer ring over the pincushion. It should fit snugly. If desired, attach the pincushion to the outer ring with a few small beads of hot glue.

Finishing

1 Hot glue a length of decorative ribbon around metal ring, starting at the back of the cat's head.

2 Finish gluing so that ends of the ribbon overlap slightly. Trim the excess from the ends. Seal the ends either by melting with a cigarette lighter (appropriate only for synthetic materials) or by running a small bead of Fray Check over the ends.

Fill the jar with some of your favorite notions or a yummy treat and gift to your cat-loving quilty friends!

Wedge

Ear

Nose

Base

Get Your Paws Off the Table Runner

FINISHED TABLE RUNNER: 18″ × 60″

Normally, I don't allow my kitties on the table. But I'm throwing caution to the wind with this table runner! Two of my favorite things—kitties and sunflowers—"mew-nite" in this beautiful table runner that combines traditional and foundation paper piecing.

MATERIALS

Note: Amounts listed are approximations. Amounts may vary depending on method used for foundation paper piecing.

LOW-VOLUME PRINT 1: 1 yard for background

LOW-VOLUME PRINT 2: ½ yard for border

GRAY PRINT 1: ¼ yard for border

GRAY PRINT 2: ¼ yard for border

YELLOW PRINT 1: 1 fat quarter for kitty blocks

GREEN PRINT: 1 fat quarter for kitty blocks

YELLOW PRINT 2: 1 fat quarter for sunflower blocks

SMALL-SCALE GREEN PRINTS: 4 fat eighths for sunflower blocks

BINDING: ½ yard

BACKING: 2 yards

BATTING: 26″ × 68″

FOUNDATION PAPER OR LIGHTWEIGHT COPY PAPER

ADD-A-QUARTER RULER

Pieced by Pamela Jane Morgan, quilted by Rob Dickinson (@roboquilter).

Cutting

Low–volume print 1

• Cut 5 strips 1½″ × width of fabric; subcut into 10 rectangles 1½″ × 3½″, 8 rectangles 1½″ × 8½″, and 8 rectangles 1½″ × 10½″.

• Use the remainder for foundation paper piecing.

Low–volume print 2

• Cut 4 strips 2½″ × width of fabric.

Gray print 1

• Cut 2 strips 2½″ × width of fabric.

Gray print 2

• Cut 2 strips 2½″ × width of fabric.

Small-scale green prints

• Cut a total of 16 squares 1½″ × 1½″. Use the remainder for foundation paper piecing.

Binding

• Cut 5 strips 2¼″ × width of fabric.

Construction

Piece the Kitties

1 Make 5 copies each of foundation patterns A–G (page 77). Due to the complexity of these blocks, making color copies will help you succeed with color placement.

2 Referring to Foundation Paper Piecing Like a Purr-fessional (page 19), foundation paper piece 5 each of sections A–G in numerical order.

3 Remove the paper foundation from sections D and E. Sew together.

4 Sew a background rectangle 1½″ × 3½″ to the front edge of kitty unit DE.

5 Repeat Steps 3 and 4 with sections F and G.

6 Remove the paper foundation from sections A, B, and C. Sew together.

7 Complete each Kitty block by joining the units as shown in the Kitty block assembly diagram. Make 5 Kitty blocks. **A**

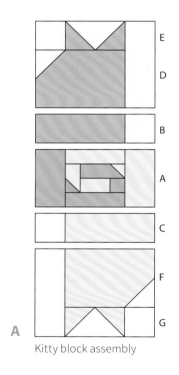

A

Kitty block assembly

Piece the Sunflowers

1 Arrange 4 small-scale green print squares 1½″ × 1½″ into a four-patch unit. Sew the squares into rows. Press in opposite directions. Join the rows, nesting the seams. Press. Make 4. **B**

2 Make 4 copies each of foundation patterns H–O (pages 78 and 79). Referring to Foundation Paper Piecing Like a Purr-fessional (page 19), foundation paper piece 4 each of sections H–O in numerical order.

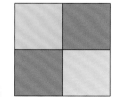

B

3 Remove the paper foundation from all the sections.

4 Join sections H, I, and J. Press the seams to the right.

5 Join section K, a four-patch unit, and section L. Press the seams to the left.

6 Join sections M, N, and O. Press the seams to the right.

7 Arrange and sew the 3 sections together, nesting the seams. Press. Make 4 Sunflower blocks.

8 Sew a background rectangle 1½″ × 8½″ to the sides of each Sunflower block. Press the seams to the background rectangle.

9 Sew a background rectangle 1½″ × 10½″ to the top and bottom of each Sunflower block. Press to the background rectangle. **C**

Make the Borders

1 Sew the low-volume print 2 strips to the gray print 1 and 2 strips to make 4 strip sets. Press the seams to the gray strips.

2 Subcut sections 2½″ × 4½″ from each strip set. Cut 15 from each strip set for a total of 30 from each gray print. **D**

3 Arrange and sew the sections together to make four-patch units. Press. Make 30. **E**

4 Join 15 four-patch units to form each border. Make 2. Press. **F**

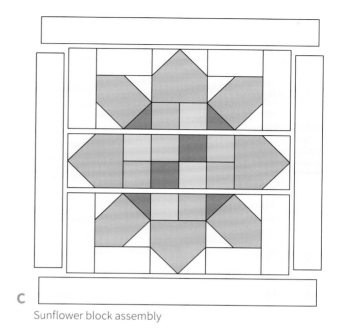

C

Sunflower block assembly

D

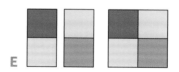

E

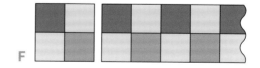

F

Assemble the Table Runner

1 Arrange and sew the Kitty and Sunflower blocks in a row, alternating the blocks. Press the seams open.

2 Sew the border rows to the long edges of the joined blocks. Press the seams open.

Finishing

Layer, baste, and quilt as desired. Bind to finish.

Table runner assembly

Cookies by Lisa Peterson (@fancifulsweets)

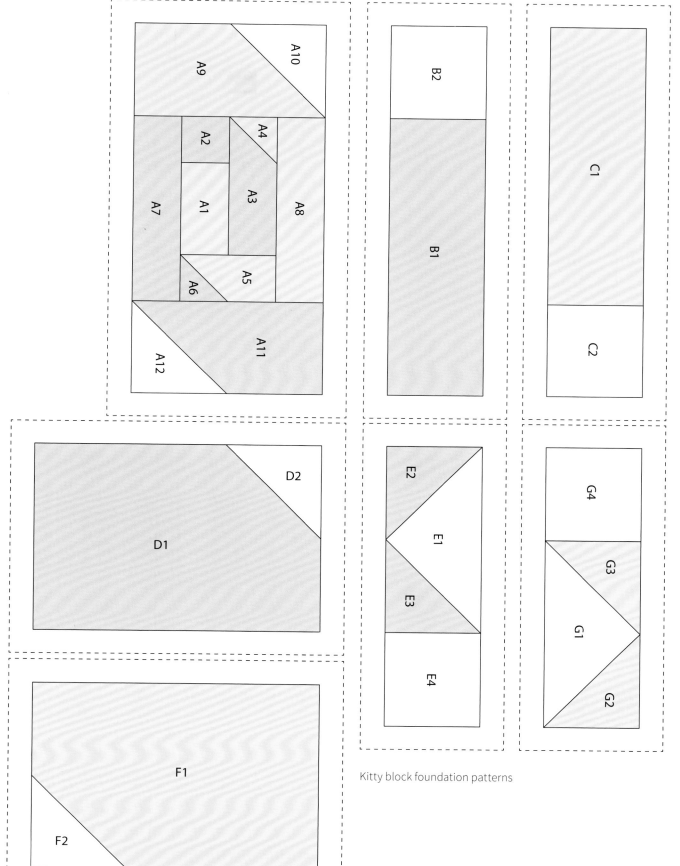

Kitty block foundation patterns

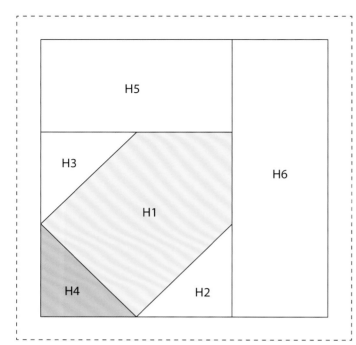

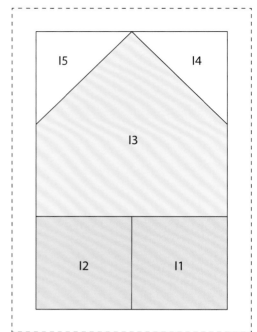

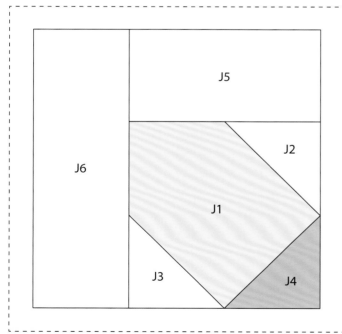

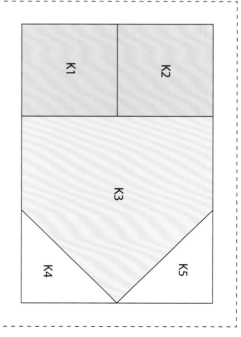

Sunflower block foundation patterns

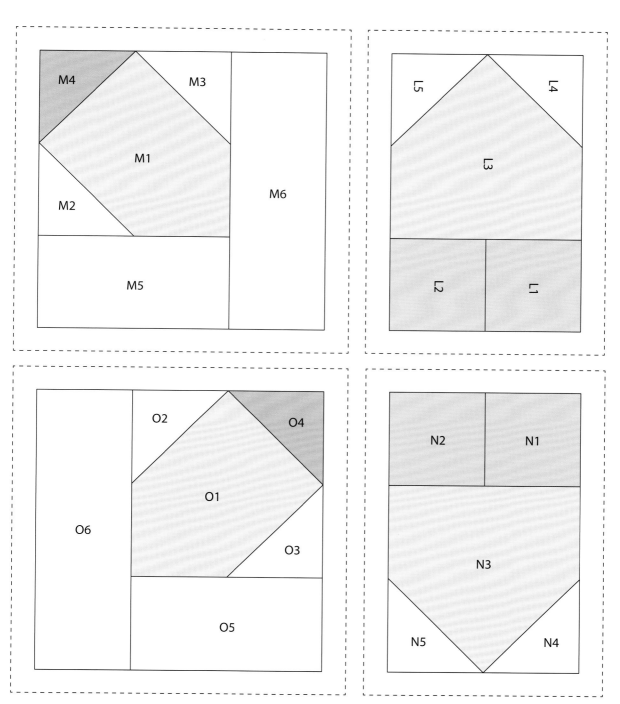

Sunflower block foundation patterns

Just Kitten Around Pillow

FINISHED PILLOW: 16″ diameter

Are you sick of cat puns yet? "Meow" neither! One of my favorite parts of writing this book was coming up with all the punny names. So of course I had to make something that was round, if not purely to be able to say that I was "just kitten' around!" And even though this project is beginner friendly, you won't be "disa-paw-nted" by the adorable design.

MATERIALS

COTTON PRINTS: 6 fat eighths for wedges

COORDINATING PRINT 1: 1 fat quarter for wedges, ears, and covered button

COORDINATING PRINT 2: ½ yard for wedges and pillow back

WHITE SOLID: ½ yard for pillow interior

FUSIBLE FLEECE: ½ yard *or* 18″ × 18″ scrap of low-loft batting

FUSIBLE FOAM INTERFACING: ⅛ yard for ears

TEMPLATE PLASTIC

ROUND PILLOW FORM: 16″ diameter

COVERED BUTTON: ½″ for nose

BUTTONS: 2, 1″ diameter for eyes

BUTTON WITH 2 HOLES: ½″–1″ for tufting

LONG UPHOLSTERY NEEDLE: 8″–10″

PERLE COTTON

FRAY CHECK (*optional*)

Cutting

Template plastic

• Trace and cut the wedge and ear patterns (page 85).

Cotton and coordinating prints

• Cut 1 from *each* print using the wedge pattern.

• Cut 4 from coordinating print 1 using the ear pattern.

White solid, fusible fleece, and coordinating print 2

• Cut 1 square 18″ × 18″ from *each*.

Fusible foam interfacing

• Cut 2 using the ear pattern.

Construction

Join the Wedges

1 Layer 2 wedge pieces right sides together. Sew together on the long straight edges. Press the seam open. **A**

2 Continue piecing in this manner to make 2 half-circle units with 4 wedges each. **B**

3 Layer the 2 half-circles right sides together and sew on the straight edge. Press the seam open. **C**

Finish the Pillow Front

1 Fuse the fleece to the wrong side of the pieced circle. Layer on top of the white solid square. Quilt as desired.

2 Trim the excess material from around the circle's edge.

3 Place the quilted circle on top of the coordinating print 2 square 18″ × 18″ and trim around the circle to cut the pillow back.

Make the Ears

1 Fuse a foam interfacing ear piece to a fabric ear piece, following manufacturer's instructions. Repeat with another ear piece from each.

2 Place the remaining fabric ear pieces on top of the fused pieces, right sides together. Sew with a ¼″ seam allowance around the outside edges, leaving the bottom edge of the pieces *open*.

3 Trim the points, being careful not to clip too close to the stitching (see Just a Little Off the Top, page 25).

4 Turn the ears right side out through the bottom. Press. Topstitch a ¼″ around the outside of the pieces. **D**

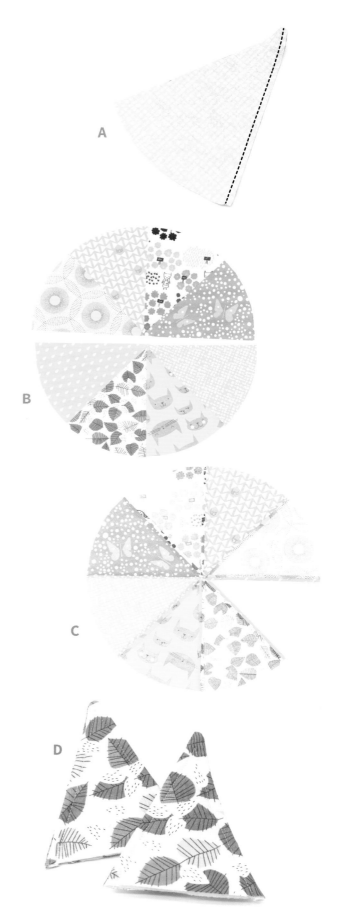

A

B

C

D

Attach the Ears

Position the pieced circle so that one wedge is at the top middle position. Place the ears on the right side of the circle with the raw edges aligned. Baste the ears in place by stitching a scant ⅛″ from the edges. **E**

Finishing

1 Measure 1″ above the center and then 1½″ to both the right and left of the center, and mark the eye placement. Using a needle and perle cotton, stitch the buttons for the eyes over the markings. **F**

2 Layer the back circle and the pillow front right sides together. Sew together, leaving a 6″–8″ opening at the bottom for turning.

3 Clip V-shaped notches in the seam allowance of the circle, taking care not to clip through the stitching. These notches will help eliminate a puckered appearance when the pillow is turned right side out (see Learn to Love Your Curves, page 25).

4 Turn the pillow right side out through the opening. Shape and press, paying special attention to the ears. Stuff the pillow form through the opening. Whipstitch the opening closed.

5 Following the package instructions, cover the 1½″ button with a scrap from coordinating print 1.

6 Thread a long length of perle cotton through a long upholstery needle. Do not knot the end. Find the center of the pillow back. Thread the needle through the 2-hole button and all the way through the pillow, leaving a thread tail on the back of the pillow. Slide the covered button shank over the needle. **G**

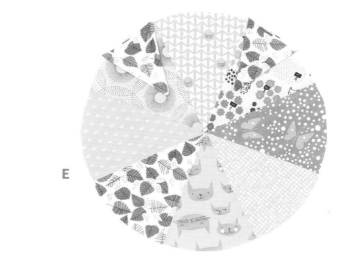

E

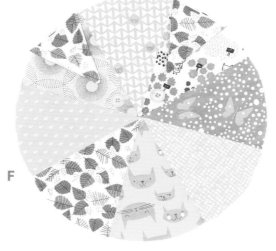

F

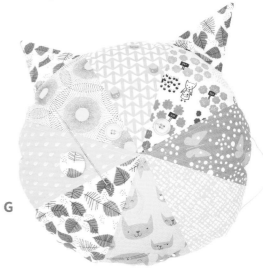

G

7 Pull the needle back through the pillow and through the holes of the button on the back of the pillow. Repeat 2 or 3 more times. On the last pull through to the back, remove the needle from the thread and leave the long tail. **H**

8 Pull the threads taut to tuft the pillow and tie a double knot. Trim the thread ends so that only a small tail remains. If desired, seal the ends with Fray Check. **I**

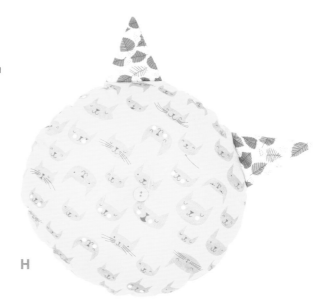

H

I

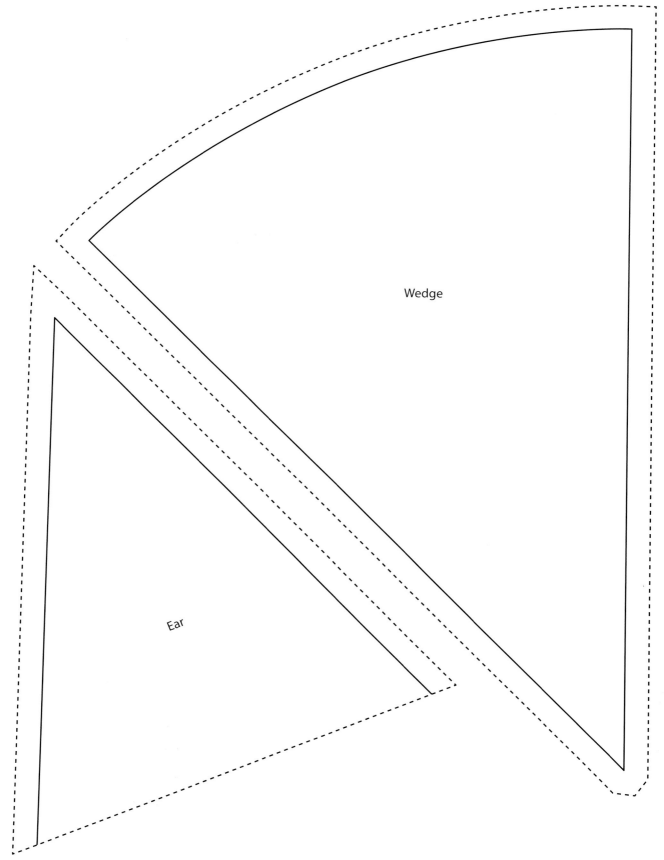

Wedge

Ear

Cat Nap Pillows

FINISHED PILLOW 1: 14″ × 14″ • FINISHED PILLOW 2: 16″ × 16″

I know I'm not supposed to play favorites, but I'm breaking all the rules—because these pillows are my favorite! This dreamy pair of pillows combines scrappy foundation paper-pieced backgrounds with delicate wool appliqué and hand embroidery. One pillow is beginner friendly, while the other is decidedly more intricate. Make one or make both! Either way, you'll be dreaming of catnaps in fields of flowers.

PILLOW 1

MATERIALS

GRAY PRINTS: A variety of medium-to-large scraps for background

GRAY SOLID: ½ yard for pillow interior

CORAL HAND-DYED WOOL: 8″ × 8″ piece for cat

DEEP PINK HAND-DYED WOOL: 6″ × 6″ piece for flowers

MUSTARD HAND-DYED WOOL: 2″ × 2″ piece for flower centers

DEEP TURQUOISE HAND-DYED WOOL: 5″ × 5″ piece for flower

AQUA WOOL-BLEND FELT: 2″ × 2″ piece for flower center

GRASS GREEN WOOL-BLEND FELT: 6″ × 6″ piece for grass

BRIGHT GREEN HAND-DYED WOOL: 2″ × 2″ piece for leaves

SMALL-SCALE GRAY PRINT: ½ yard for pillow back

LOW-LOFT BATTING: 18″ × 18″

PAPER-BACKED FUSIBLE WEB: ½ yard

PERLE COTTON OR EMBROIDERY FLOSS in coordinating colors

FOUNDATION PAPER OR LIGHTWEIGHT COPY PAPER

PILLOW FORM: 14″ × 14″

BAMBOO POINT TURNER (*optional*)

Cutting

Gray solid

• Cut 1 square 18″ × 18″.

Small–scale gray print

• Cut 2 pieces 14½″ × 19½″.

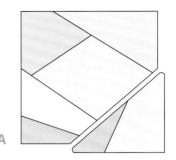

A

Construction

Piece the Blocks

1 Make 4 copies each of foundation patterns A and B (next page and page 90). Use tape to connect the 2 sections of foundation pattern A, matching the broken lines. Referring to Foundation Paper Piecing Like a Purr-fessional (page 19), foundation paper piece all sections. Remove the foundation paper.

2 Join sections A and B, right sides together. Press the seam open. Repeat to make 4 AB units. **A**

3 Rotate the 4 AB units until you're pleased with their arrangement. Sew into rows, pressing the seams in opposite directions. Join the rows, nesting the seams. Press. **B**

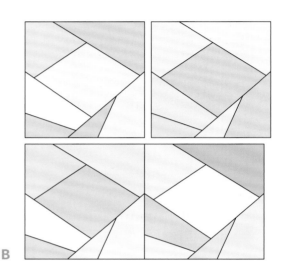

B

Appliqué and Embroider

1 Enlarge the appliqué patterns (page 91) to 200%. Trace onto paper-backed fusible web. Cut and fuse to the wool pieces referring to Raw-Edge Appliqué (page 22).

2 Arrange the appliqué motifs on the pieced background referring to the stitch and placement diagram. Fuse and then stitch in place, either by hand or machine.

3 Transfer the embroidery designs using your desired method, referring to the stitch and placement diagram. Complete the embroidery. **C**

Backstitch

Backstitch

Stem Stitch

C

Stitch and placement

Finishing

1 Layer the appliquéd pillow front, batting, and a gray solid square. Quilt as desired. Trim the quilted pillow front to 14½″ × 14½″.

2 To make the pillow back, press each small-scale gray piece in half so that they each measure 9¾″ × 14½″. Topstitch 1″ from the folds. **D**

3 With the pillow front right side up, layer the back pieces on top with the raw edges aligned. The folded edges will overlap one another by several inches. Pin in place.

4 Stitch around the outer edge of the pillow, backstitching at the beginning and end. **E**

5 Turn the pillow right side out through the overlap. Push the corners outward using a bamboo point turner or similar object. Press. Insert the pillow form through the opening in the back.

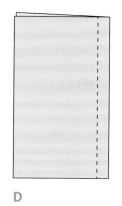

D

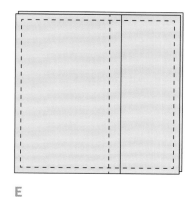

E

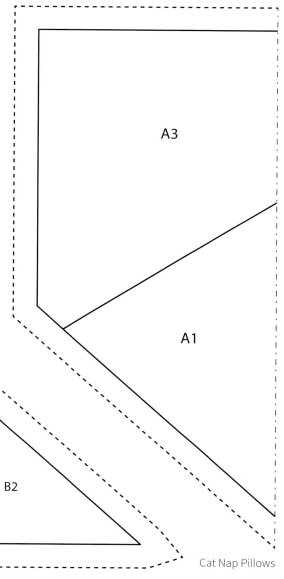

A3

A1

B1

B2

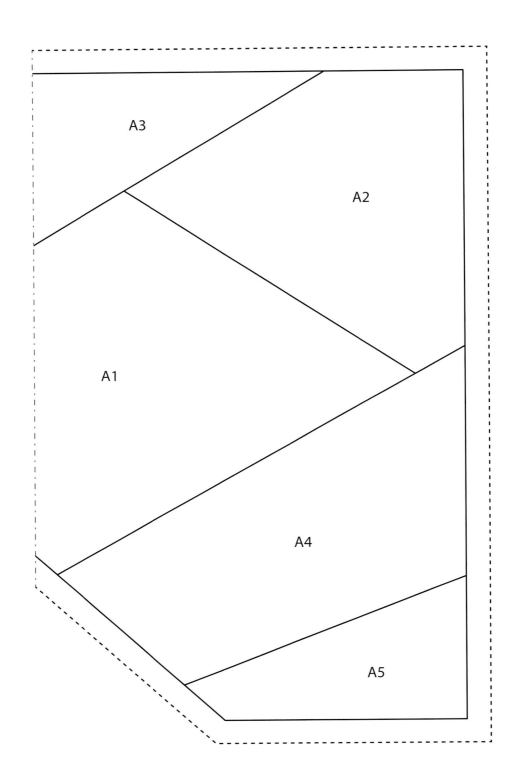

A3

A2

A1

A4

A5

Enlarge appliqué patterns to 200%.

PILLOW 2

MATERIALS

GRAY PRINTS: A variety of small-to-medium scraps for background

GRAY SOLID: ⅝ yard for pillow interior

DARK CORAL HAND-DYED WOOL: 6″ × 10″ piece for cat

LIGHT CORAL WOOL-BLEND FELT: 3″ × 6″ piece for cat details

CORAL HAND-DYED WOOL: 6″ × 6″ piece for flowers

WHITE WOOL-BLEND FELT: 4″ × 4″ for flower centers

FUCHSIA WOOL-BLEND FELT: 6″ × 9″ piece for flower petals

MUSTARD HAND-DYED WOOL: 4″ × 4″ piece for flower centers

AQUA WOOL-BLEND FELT: 6″ × 9″ piece for flowers

TURQUOISE HAND-DYED WOOL: 5″ × 5″ piece for flower centers

LAVENDER HAND-DYED WOOL: 5″ × 5″ piece for floral appliqué

BRIGHT GREEN HAND-DYED WOOL: 6″ × 6″ piece for leaves

GRASS GREEN WOOL-BLEND FELT: 6″ × 9″ piece for stems and leaves

SMALL-SCALE GRAY PRINT: ½ yard for pillow back

LOW-LOFT BATTING: 20″ × 20″

PAPER-BACKED FUSIBLE WEB: ½ yard

PERLE COTTON OR EMBROIDERY FLOSS in coordinating colors

FOUNDATION PAPER OR LIGHTWEIGHT COPY PAPER

PILLOW FORM: 16″ × 16″

BAMBOO POINT TURNER (*optional*)

Cutting

Gray solid
• Cut 1 square 20″ × 20″.

Small-scale gray print
• Cut 2 pieces 16½″ × 20½″.

Construction

Piece the Blocks

1 Make 16 copies of the foundation pattern (page 94). Referring to Foundation Paper Piecing Like a Purr-fessional (page 19), foundation paper piece all sections. Remove the paper foundations.

2 Join the 4 foundation sections to make a block. Make 4 blocks.

3 Sew into rows, pressing the seams in opposite directions. Join the rows, nesting the seams. Press. **A**

Appliqué and Embroider

1 Trace the appliqué patterns (pages 94 and 95) on paper-backed fusible web. Cut and fuse to the wool pieces referring to Raw-Edge Appliqué (page 22).

2 Arrange the appliqué motifs on the pieced background referring to the stitch and placement diagram. Fuse and then stitch in place, either by hand or machine.

3 Transfer the embroidery designs using your preferred method, referring to the stitch placement diagram. **B**

Finishing

1 Layer appliquéd pillow front, batting, and gray solid square. Quilt as desired. Trim the quilted pillow front to 16½″ × 16½″.

2 To make the pillow back, press each small-scale gray piece in half so that they each measure 10¼″ × 16½″. Topstitch 1″ from the folds.

3 Refer to Pillow 1, Finishing, Steps 3–5 (page 89) to complete the pillow.

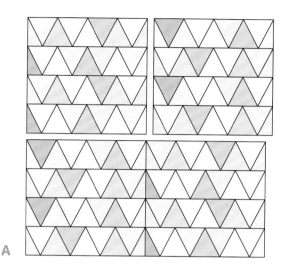

A

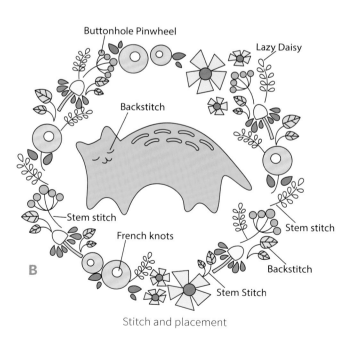

B

Stitch and placement

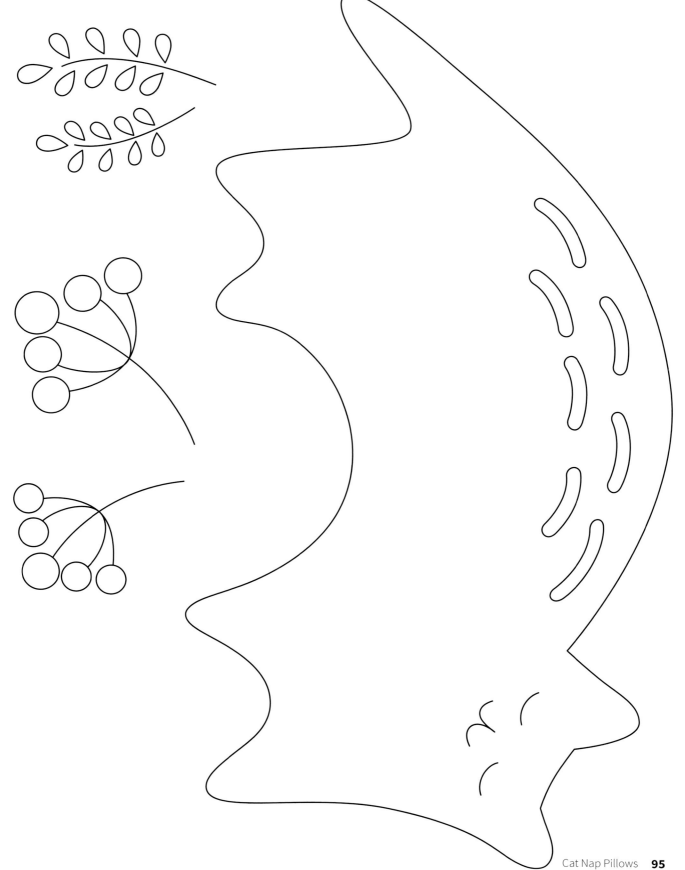

Self Pawtrait Pillow/Softie

FINISHED SOFTIE: 10″ wide × 15″ high × 3″ deep

My original inspiration for this project was seeing a beautiful antique Dresden Plate quilt that had been cut up and turned into a stuffed cat. I'm always saddened to see these gorgeous, timeworn works of art being cut into. Why cut up someone else's work when it's so easy to make your own? This simple-to-make work of art will be cherished by your family (fur or human) for years to come. It would make a wonderful gift for a cat-loving child. Or sprinkle a little catnip in with the stuffing and make a partner for your real kitty to love on!

MATERIALS

QUILTER'S LINEN: ½ yard for body and tail

SMALL-SCALE PRINTS: 11 scraps 4″ × 4″ for Dresden Plate petals and center

LIGHT PINK WOOL-BLEND FELT: 1″ × 1″ scrap for nose

POLYESTER FIBERFILL STUFFING

BUTTONS: 2, ⅝″ diameter for eyes

TEMPLATE PLASTIC

FREEZER PAPER OR SCRAP OF PAPER-BACKED FUSIBLE WEB

BAMBOO POINT TURNER (*optional*)

Cutting

Patterns

- Trace and cut the dresden plate petal pattern (page 101) using template plastic.
- Enlarge the body and tail patterns (page 100) 200%.

Quilter's linen

- Cut 2 body and 2 tail pieces using the enlarged patterns.

Small-scale prints

- Cut 10 using the petal pattern.
- Trace the center pattern (page 101) on freezer paper or fusible web. Fuse to the fabric and cut 1.

Construction

Make the Dresden Plate Arc

1 Fold each Dresden plate petal in half lengthwise, right sides together. Stitch the top edge, backstitching at the beginning and end of the seam. **A**

2 Turn the petals right side out. If necessary, use a bamboo point turner to help bring the points outward. Press. **B**

3 Place 2 petals right sides together and sew together on the long edge. Press the seam open. **C**

4 Repeat until all 10 petals are sewn together in pairs. Join together in an arc. Press the seams open. **D**

A   B

C

D

Assemble the Cat Front

1 Position the Dresden plate arc on the left side of the front cat-body piece, right sides up. Pin in place; then topstitch close to the folded edges of the petals.

2 Position the prepared center circle, overlapping the raw edges of the petals. About half of the circle will overhang the edge of the cat body. Remove the paper backing or freezer paper, and fuse or glue baste in place. Appliqué using a machine satin stitch or blanket stitch. Trim the excess fabric so that the edges of the Dresden Plate are flush with the edge of the cat body. **E**

3 Trace the nose pattern on a small scrap of paper-backed fusible web; then fuse to the light pink wool-blend felt. Cut out and remove the paper backing. Fold and finger-press the cat front to find the center. Position the nose on the center crease 2¼″ from the top of the cat's head. Sew the nose in place close to the edges.

4 Position the eye buttons ¾″ on either side of the nose, aligning with the top edge of the nose. Sew in place. **F**

TIP *I used buttons that had a cat's eye shape in the center. They are easily found in the carded buttons at most major fabric and craft retailers.*

5 Position a tail piece so that it's 1¾″ from the bottom right edge of the front cat-body piece. With right sides together, sew in place, backstitching at the beginning and end. Press the seam toward the tail. Repeat with the remaining tail and body pieces, positioning the tail on the bottom left edge. **G**

Finishing

1 Place the completed cat pieces right sides together. Pin and sew around the outer edges, leaving a 4″ opening in the bottom for turning. **H**

2 Clip the curves, being careful not to cut through the stitching (see Learn to Love Your Curves, page 25). Turn right side out through the opening in the bottom.

3 Fill with fiberfill, using the eraser end of a pencil to help push stuffing into the tail and ears.

4 Whipstitch the opening closed with coordinating thread.

Note The petal arc will hang slightly over the edge of the cat body. This will be trimmed even with the edges in a later step.

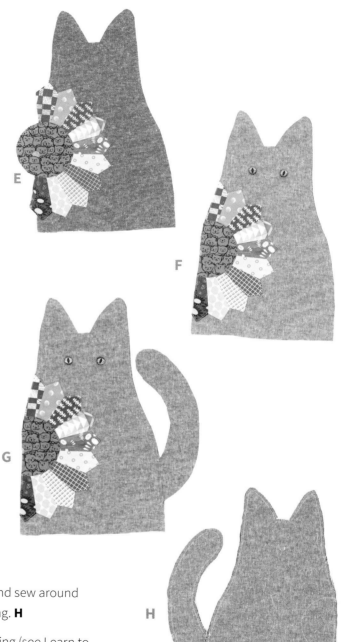

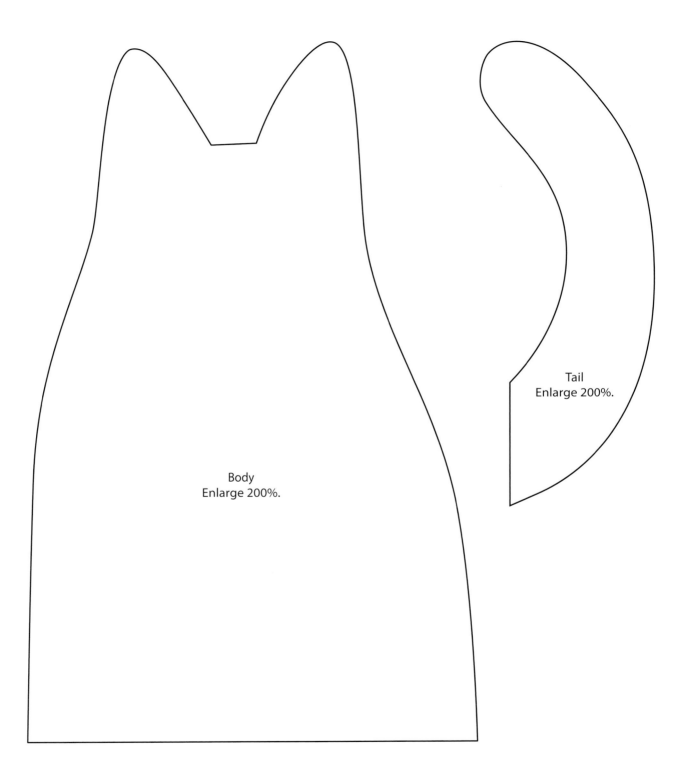

Body
Enlarge 200%.

Tail
Enlarge 200%.

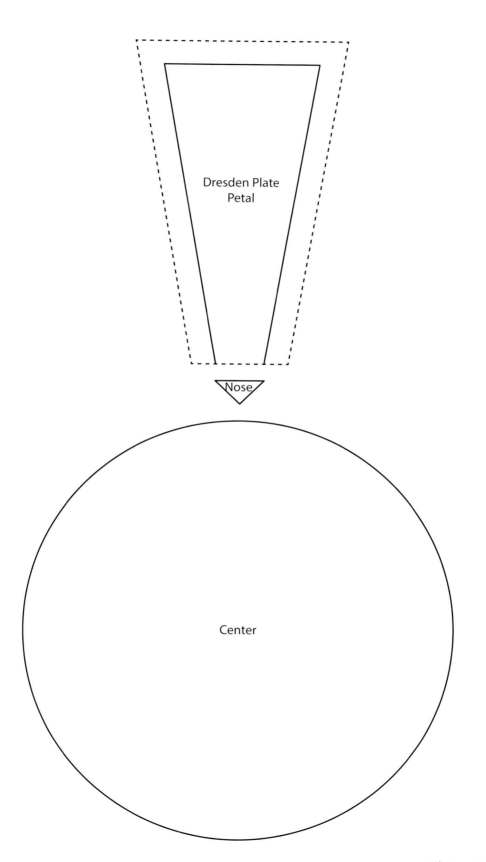

Dresden Plate
Petal

Nose

Center

Blooming Curiosity Quilt

FINISHED QUILT: 84″ × 84″

We all know the saying about cats and curiosity. Lucky for us, our fur babies have nine lives. Still, I prefer when my kitties exercise their curiosity by smelling the pretty flowers, watching the birds out our large picture windows, or playing hide-and-seek behind the many quilt ladders in our home.

Though this quilt is the largest in the book, it's one of the quickest to make thanks to the use of precut 10″ squares. Let your creative curiosity bloom while you experiment with this fabulous quilt!

Pieced by Pamela Jane Morgan, quilted by Christy Christensen (@6littlestitches)

MATERIALS

LOW-VOLUME PRINT: ½ yard for medallion background

WHITE PRINT: Small scrap for flower center

TURQUOISE PRINT 1: ⅛ yard for flower

TURQUOISE PRINT 2: ⅛ yard for flower

GREEN PRINT: ⅛ yard for leaves and stem

DARK PINK PRINT 1: ⅛ yard for flower

DARK PINK PRINT 2: ⅛ yard for flower

DARK PINK PRINT 3: ⅛ yard for flower

GREEN SOLID: ⅛ yard for leaves and stem

MEDIUM-SCALE AQUA/PINK PRINT: 1 fat quarter for cat

MEDIUM-SCALE GREEN PRINT: ⅜ yard for medallion grass

STRIPED PRINT: 1 yard for medallion border and binding

PRECUT 10″ SQUARES: 72 *or* 2 precut 10″ square packs for disappearing Nine-Patch blocks

BACKING: 9 yards or 3 yards of 108″-wide backing

BATTING: 90″ × 90″

Cutting

Note: *Directionality of fabric is important in the center medallion. All cuts are listed as width × length.*

Flower unit

LOW-VOLUME PRINT

• Cut 1 rectangle 11½″ × 7½″.

Flower 1

LOW-VOLUME PRINT

• Cut 1 strip 2″ × width of fabric; subcut into 2 rectangles 2″ × 2½″ and 4 squares 1″ × 1″.

• Cut 1 strip 1¼″ × width of fabric; subcut into 2 rectangles 1¼″ × 7½″ and 4 squares 1¼″ × 1¼″.

WHITE PRINT

• Cut 1 square 2½″ × 2½″.

TURQUOISE PRINT 1

• Cut 2 rectangles 1¼″ × 2½″.

TURQUOISE PRINT 2

• Cut 2 rectangles 4″ × 1¼″.

GREEN PRINT

• Cut 1 square 2¾″ × 2¾″.

GREEN SOLID

• Cut 1 rectangle 1″ × 4″ and 1 square 2¾″ × 2¾″.

Flower 2

LOW-VOLUME PRINT

• Cut 1 strip 1½″ × width of fabric; subcut into 2 rectangles 1½″ × 4″ and 4 squares 1½″ × 1½″.

• Cut 2 squares 3¼″ × 3¼″.

• Cut 2 rectangles 3¼″ × 2″.

• Cut 1 square 2¼″ × 2¼″.

• Cut 2 rectangles 1¼″ × 2½″.

DARK PINK PRINT 1

• Cut 1 square 2¼″ × 2¼″.

• Cut 1 rectangle 2½″ × 1½″.

DARK PINK PRINT 2

• Cut 1 rectangle 4½″ × 2″.

DARK PINK PRINT 3

• Cut 1 rectangle 4½″ × 1½″.

GREEN SOLID

• Cut 1 square 3¼″ × 3¼″.

• Cut 1 rectangle 1″ × 4″.

Cat unit

LOW-VOLUME PRINT

• Cut 1 rectangle 6½″ × 4″.

• Cut 1 square 5½″ × 5½″.

• Cut 1 rectangle 4″ × 6½″.

• Cut 1 rectangle 2½″ × 6½″.

• Cut 2 squares 2½″ × 2½″.

• Cut 3 squares 2″ × 2″.

• Cut 2 rectangles 1½″ × 14½″.

MEDIUM-SCALE AQUA/PINK PRINT

• Cut 1 rectangle 6½″ × 11″.

• Cut 2 rectangles 5½″ × 2″.

• Cut 1 rectangle 2½″ × 8½″.

• Cut 1 rectangle 2″ × 6½″.

• Cut 2 squares 2″ × 2″.

MEDIUM-SCALE GREEN PRINT

• Cut 1 rectangle 26½″ × 12½″.

Border and binding

STRIPED PRINT

• Cut 4 strips 1½″ × WOF; subcut into 2 pieces 1½″ × 26½″ and 2 pieces 28½″ × 1½″.

• Cut 10 strips 2¼″ × width of fabric for the binding.

Construction

Piece Flower 1

Press all seams open unless otherwise instructed. Pay close attention to the orientation of the seams in the half-square triangles as you assemble the flower and leaf units.

1 With right sides together, sew 2 turquoise print 1 rectangles 1¼″ × 2½″ to opposite sides of the white print square.

2 Sew 2 turquoise print 2 rectangles 4″ × 1¼″ to the top and bottom of the white print square.

3 Draw a diagonal line on the wrong side of 4 low-volume print squares 1¼″ × 1¼″. With right sides together, place the marked square on a corner of the unit. Sew on the drawn line and trim the seam allowance to ¼″. Press.

4 Repeat Step 3 with the remaining low-volume print squares 1¼″ × 1¼″ to complete the flower head. **A**

5 To make the leaf units, draw a diagonal line on the wrong side of the green print square 2¾″ × 2¾″. Layer the marked square and the green solid square 2¾″ × 2¾″ right sides together. Sew a scant ¼″ seam on each side of the drawn line (see Two-at-a-Time Stitch-and-Flip Piecing, page 9).

6 Cut in half on the drawn line and press. Trim each half-square triangle to 2″ × 2″ (see Square It Up, page 10).

7 Draw a diagonal line on the wrong side of the 4 low-volume print squares 1″ × 1″. Place on the corners of the units from Step 6, right sides together, so that the drawn lines are parallel to the center seam. Sew on the drawn lines. Trim the seam allowances to ¼″ (see Stitch-and-Flip Piecing, page 8). **B**

8 Sew a low-volume print rectangle 2″ × 2½″ to the top edge of each leaf unit.

9 Sew the leaf units to both sides of the green solid rectangle 1″ × 4″.

10 Sew the flower head unit to the top edge of the leaf-and-stem unit.

11 Sew a 1¼″ × 7½″ rectangle to each side of flower 1. **C**

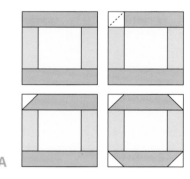

A

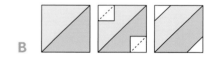

B

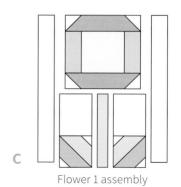

C

Flower 1 assembly

Piece Flower 2

Press all seams open unless otherwise instructed. Pay close attention to the orientation of the seams in the half-square triangles as you assemble the flower and leaf units.

1 Draw a diagonal line on the wrong side of a low-volume print square 2¼″ × 2¼″. Layer right sides together with a dark pink print 1 square 2¼″ × 2¼″. Sew a scant ¼″ seam on each side of the drawn line (see Two-at-a-Time Stitch-and-Flip Piecing, page 9).

2 Cut in half on the drawn line and press. Trim each half-square triangle to 1½″ × 1½″ (see Square It Up, page 10).

3 Draw a diagonal line on the wrong side of 2 low-volume squares 1½″ × 1½″. Place on the end of a dark pink print 1 rectangle 2½″ × 1½″. Sew on the drawn line and trim the seam allowance. Repeat on the other end to make a Flying Geese unit (see Stitch-and-Flip Flying Geese, page 9).

4 Sew the half-square triangles from Step 2 to the ends of the Flying Geese unit. Press.

5 Draw a diagonal line on the wrong side of 2 low-volume print squares 1½″ × 1½″. Using stitch-and-flip piecing (page 8), sew to the ends of the dark pink print 3 rectangle 4½″ × 1½″. Trim the seam allowances to ¼″.

6 Arrange and sew the units from Steps 4 and 5 to the dark pink print 2 rectangle 4½″ × 2″. Press. Sew 1 low-volume print rectangle 1½″ × 4″ to each side to complete the flower head.

7 To make the leaf units, draw a diagonal line on the wrong side of the low-volume print square 3¼″ × 3¼″. Layer the marked square and the green solid square 3¼″ × 3¼″ right sides together. Sew a scant ¼″ seam on each side of the drawn line (see Two-at-a-Time Stitch-and-Flip Piecing, page 9).

8 Cut in half on the drawn line and press. Trim each half-square triangle to 2½″ × 2½″ (see Square It Up, page 10).

9 Sew a low-volume print rectangle 1¼″ × 2½″ to one side of each leaf unit.

10 Sew a low-volume print rectangle 3¼″ × 2″ to the top of each leaf unit.

11 Sew a leaf unit to either side of the solid green rectangle 1″ × 4″. Press.

12 Sew the flower head to the leaf-and-stem unit. **D**

Finish the Flower Unit

Press all seams open.

1 With right sides together, sew flower 1 and flower 2 together. Press. **E**

2 Sew the low-volume print rectangle 11½″ × 7½″ to the top of the flower unit.

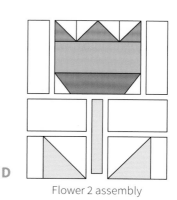

D

Flower 2 assembly

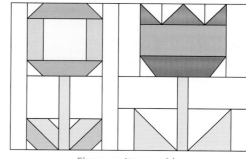

E

Flower unit assembly

Piece the Cat Unit

1 Use the cat unit assembly diagram as a guide for placement. Press all seams open. For detailed piecing instructions, see One Cat Leads to Another (page 10).

2 Complete the cat unit by sewing low-volume print rectangles 1½″ × 14½″ to the sides of the cat unit. Press. **F**

Finish the Medallion

Press all seams open unless otherwise specified.

1 Sew the flower and cat units together. Press. Join to the medium-scale green print rectangle. **G**

2 Sew the striped border pieces 1½″ × 26½″ to the sides of the medallion. Press the seams toward the border.

3 Sew the striped border pieces 28½″ × 1½″ to the top and bottom of the medallion. Press the seams toward the border.

Make the Disappearing Nine-Patch Blocks

1 For each Nine-Patch block, arrange 9 different precut 10″ squares into 3 rows of 3 squares each.

2 Sew the squares into rows. Press.

3 Join the rows. Press.

4 Make 8 Nine-Patch blocks. Each block should measure 29″ from raw edge to raw edge. **H**

5 Transforming the Nine-Patch blocks to disappearing Nine-Patch blocks is simple! Cut each block in half lengthwise and then widthwise. The result should be 32 blocks measuring 14½″ × 14½″, including seam allowances. **I**

TIP *Most quilting rulers aren't longer than 24″ in length. This obviously poses a problem when cutting these large blocks in half. The solution? Press each block in half, both lengthwise and widthwise. Then cut along the pressed lines.*

F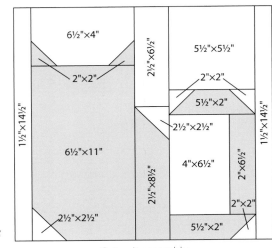

Cat unit assembly

G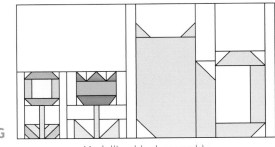

Medallion block assembly

H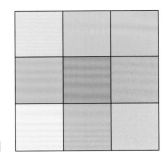

I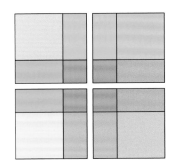

Assemble the Quilt Top

1 Using a design wall or flat surface, arrange the blocks in 6 rows of 6 blocks each, with the medallion replacing 4 blocks in rows 3 and 4. In the odd-numbered rows (1, 3, 5), the orientation of the blocks will follow pattern A and B. **J**

2 In the even-numbered rows (2, 4, 6), the orientation of the blocks will follow pattern C and D. **K**

3 For rows 1 and 2, sew 6 blocks together for each row. Press. Join the rows. Press. Repeat for rows 5 and 6.

4 For rows 3 and 4, sew 2 blocks together for each partial row. Press. Join the partial rows. Press. Sew to the sides of the center medallion. Press.

5 Sew the 3 groups of rows together. Press.

Finishing

Layer the backing, batting, and quilt top. Baste and quilt as desired. Finish with a label and binding.

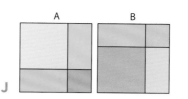

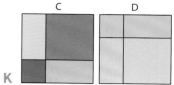

Quilt top assembly

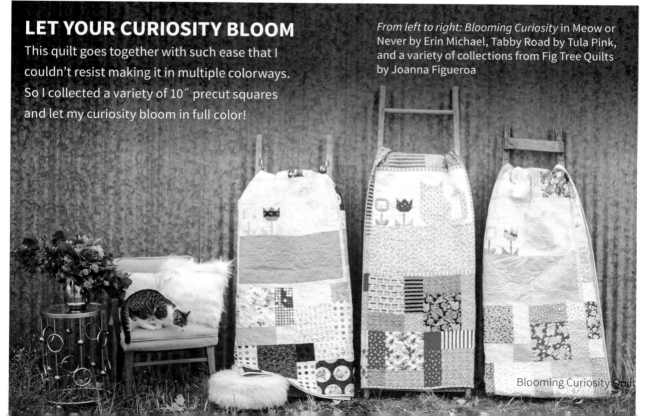

LET YOUR CURIOSITY BLOOM

This quilt goes together with such ease that I couldn't resist making it in multiple colorways. So I collected a variety of 10˝ precut squares and let my curiosity bloom in full color!

From left to right: Blooming Curiosity in Meow or Never by Erin Michael, Tabby Road by Tula Pink, and a variety of collections from Fig Tree Quilts by Joanna Figueroa

Feline Floral Quilt

FINISHED QUILT: 62″ × 65″

Feline Floral *was born of a desire to create a smaller version of the* Blooming Curiosity Quilt. *This quilt also calls for precut squares, which allow for a wide variety of fabric prints and colors. They also make assembly a breeze! The flower and cat blocks require slightly more intricate piecing, but the majority of the quilt is comprised of disappearing Nine-Patch blocks, just like* Blooming Curiosity.

MATERIALS

WHITE SOLID: ¾ yard for background

SMALL-SCALE PINK PRINT: ½ yard for Flower blocks

NAVY PRINT: 1 fat quarter for flower centers

SMALL-SCALE GREEN PRINT: 1 fat quarter for stems and leaves

PINK FLORAL PRINT: 1 fat quarter for Cat block

PRECUT 5″ SQUARES: 171 for disappearing Nine-Patch blocks

BINDING: ⅝ yard

BACKING: 4 yards

BATTING: 70″ × 73″

Pieced by Pamela Jane Morgan, Daniel Morgan, and Charisma Horton;
quilted by Charisma Horton (@charismahorton)

Cutting

Flower blocks

WHITE SOLID

- Cut 6 strips 2″ × width of fabric; subcut 2 strips into 40 squares 2″ × 2″. Subcut 4 strips into 20 rectangles 2″ × 7″.
- Cut 3 strips 1¼″ × width of fabric; subcut into 80 squares 1¼″ × 1¼″.
- Cut 2 strips 1″ × width of fabric; subcut into 80 squares 1″ × 1″.

SMALL-SCALE PINK PRINT

- Cut 7 strips 1¼″ × width of fabric. Subcut 4 strips into 40 rectangles 4″ × 1¼″. Subcut 3 strips into 40 rectangles 2½″ × 1¼″.

NAVY PRINT

- Cut 20 squares 2½″ × 2½″.

SMALL-SCALE GREEN PRINT

- Cut 4 strips 2″ × width of fabric; subcut into 40 squares 2″ × 2″.
- Cut 20 rectangles 1″ × 3½″.

Cat block

Directionality of fabric is important in this block. All cuts are listed as width × length.

WHITE SOLID

- Cut 1 rectangle 6½″ × 3″.
- Cut 1 rectangle 5½″ × 4½″
- Cut 1 rectangle 4″ × 6½″
- Cut 2 squares 2½″ × 2½″.
- Cut 1 rectangle 2½″ × 5½″.
- Cut 3 squares 2″ × 2″.

PINK FLORAL PRINT

- Cut 1 strip 2″ × width of fabric; subcut into 2 squares 2″ × 2″ and 2 rectangles 5½″ × 2″.
- Cut 1 rectangle 6½″ × 11″.
- Cut 1 rectangle 2½″ × 8½″.
- Cut 1 rectangle 2″ × 6½″.

Binding

- Cut 7 strips 2¼″ × width of fabric.

Construction

Make the Flower Blocks

Press all seams open unless otherwise instructed. Pay close attention to the orientation of the seams in the half-square triangles as you assemble the flower and leaf units.

FLOWER HEAD UNIT

1 With right sides together, sew 2 pink print rectangles 2½″ × 1¼″ to opposite sides of a navy print square.

2 Sew 2 pink print rectangles 4″ × 1¼″ to the top and bottom of the navy print square.

3 Draw a diagonal line on the wrong side of 4 white squares 1¼″ × 1¼″. With right sides together, place a marked square on a corner of the unit. Sew on the drawn line and trim the seam allowance to ¼″. Press.

4 Repeat Step 3 with the remaining white squares 1¼″ × 1¼″ to complete the flower head. Make 20 flower head units. **A**

A

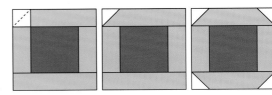

Flower head unit: Make 20.

LEAF-AND-STEM UNIT

1 Draw a diagonal line on the wrong side of 2 white squares 1″ × 1″. With right sides together, place on opposite corners of a green print square 2″ × 2″. Sew on the drawn lines and trim the seam allowances to ¼″. Press. Make 40 leaf units. **B**

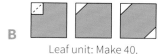

B

Leaf unit: Make 40.

2 Sew a white square 2″ × 2″ to the top of each leaf unit. Sew a leaf unit to each side of a green print rectangle 1″ × 3½″. Make 20 leaf-and-stem units.

FINISH THE FLOWER BLOCKS

1 Sew a flower head unit to each leaf-and-stem unit. Make 20 Flower blocks. **C**

2 Sew a white rectangle 2″ × 7″ to the left edge of a flower block to make flower A. Make 10 Flower A blocks. **D**

3 Sew a white rectangle 2″ × 7″ to the right edge of a Flower block to make flower B. Make 10 Flower B blocks. **E**

4 Each Flower block should measure 5½″ × 7″ with seam allowances (or 5″ × 6½″ finished).

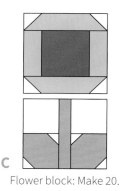

C

Flower block: Make 20.

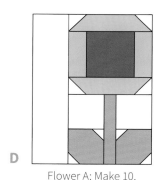

D

Flower A: Make 10.

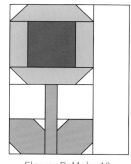

E

Flower B: Make 10.

Make the Cat Block

Press all seams open.

Use the Cat block assembly diagram as a guide for placement. For detailed piecing instructions, see One Cat Leads to Another (page 10). The block should measure 13½″ × 13½″ with seam allowances (or 13″ × 13″ finished). **F**

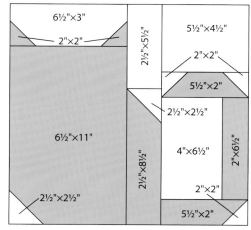

F

Cat block assembly

Make the Disappearing Nine-Patch Blocks

1 For each Nine-Patch block, arrange 9 different precut 5″ squares into 3 rows of 3 squares each.

2 Sew the squares into rows. Press.

3 Join the rows. Press.

4 Make 19 Nine-Patch blocks. Each block should measure 14″ from raw edge to raw edge. **G**

5 Transforming the Nine-Patch blocks to disappearing Nine-Patch blocks is simple! Cut each block in half lengthwise and then widthwise. The result should be 76 blocks measuring 7″ × 7″, including seam allowances. **H**

Assemble the Quilt Top

1 Using a design wall or flat surface, arrange the blocks in 10 rows of 10 blocks each, with the Cat block replacing 4 blocks in rows 5 and 6. Place the Flower blocks at the ends of the rows to create a border effect.

2 In the odd-numbered rows (1, 3, 5, 7, 9), the rows begin with a Flower A block and end with a Flower B block. The orientation of the Nine-Patch blocks will follow pattern A and B. **I**

3 In the even-numbered rows (2, 4, 6, 8, 10), the rows begin with a Flower B block and end with a Flower A block. The orientation of the Nine-Patch blocks will follow pattern C and D. **J**

4 For rows 1–4, sew the blocks together for each row. Press. Join the rows. Press. Repeat for rows 7–10.

5 For rows 5 and 6, sew 3 blocks together for each partial row. Press. Join the partial rows. Press. Sew to the sides of the cat block. Press.

6 Sew the 3 groups of rows together. Press.

Finishing

Layer the backing, batting, and quilt top. Baste and quilt as desired. Finish with a label and binding.

G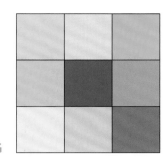

H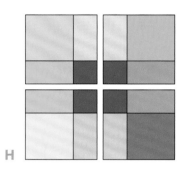

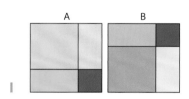

I

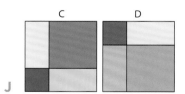

J

Quilt top assembly

Feline Floral

*W*hisker Away Quilt

FINISHED QUILT: 60″ × 60″

What's cuter than a vintage bike with an attached basket? A vintage bike with a basket that's holding a cat, that's what! A play on the Square-in-a-Square block, this fun quilt features simple piecing surrounding a whimsical free-motion embroidered block. It doesn't get much cuter than this!

MATERIALS

Note I suggest choosing nondirectional prints for this quilt. The quilt itself is very directional, and choosing fabrics with an obvious direction will make assembly more difficult.

PINK PRINT 1: 1 fat quarter for quarter-square triangles

PINK PRINT 2: 1 yard for quarter-square triangles

COORDINATING PRINTS: 15 assorted fat quarters for patchwork

QUILTER'S LINEN: 1 fat quarter for appliqué background

LIGHT PINK SOLID: 1 yard for bike and binding

BLACK SOLID: 1 fat quarter for bike

LIGHT GRAY SOLID: ⅛ yard for bike details

BURLAP FABRIC: ⅛ yard for basket

ORANGE HAND-DYED WOOL: 5″ × 5″ piece for cat

MUSTARD HAND-DYED WOOL: 2½″ × 2½″ piece for butterfly wings

BLACK HAND-DYED WOOL: 2½″ × 2½″ piece for butterfly body

PINK HAND-DYED WOOL: 2½″ × 2½″ piece for flowers

LIGHTWEIGHT WOVEN INTERFACING: ½ yard (I like Pellon's SF101 Shape-Flex.)

PAPER-BACKED FUSIBLE WEB: ½ yard

BACKING: 4 yards

BATTING: 68″ × 68″

PERLE COTTON OR 6-STRAND EMBROIDERY FLOSS

Pieced and quilted by
Pamela Jane Morgan

Cutting

Pink print 1

• Cut 1 square 16¼″ × 16¼″; subcut into quarters diagonally.

Pink print 2

• Cut 1 square 31¼″ × 31¼″; subcut into quarters diagonally.

Coordinating prints

FROM *EACH* OF THE 15 FAT QUARTERS:

• Cut 1 square 6⅞″ × 6⅞″; subcut in half diagonally.

• Cut 3 squares 6½″ × 6½″.

• Cut 1 square 3⅞″ × 3⅞″; subcut in half diagonally.

• Cut 5 squares 3½″ × 3½″.

Note **You will have extra coordinating print patches.**

Quilter's linen and lightweight woven interfacing

• Cut 1 square 15½″ × 15½″ from *each*.

Light pink solid

• Cut 7 strips 2¼″ × width of fabric for the binding.

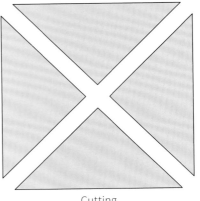

Cutting

Construction

Appliqué and Embroidery

1 Fuse the interfacing to the wrong side of the linen square.

2 Enlarge the appliqué patterns (page 119) to 200%. Trace on paper-backed fusible web. Cut and fuse to the fabrics and wool pieces, referring to Raw-Edge Appliqué (page 22).

3 Arrange the appliqué motifs on the linen square, referring to the stitch and placement diagram. Be sure to layer the bike over the tires; then layer the pedal, hand, and seat. Place the cat body, then the basket, followed by the cat paws so they overlap the basket. Fuse in place.

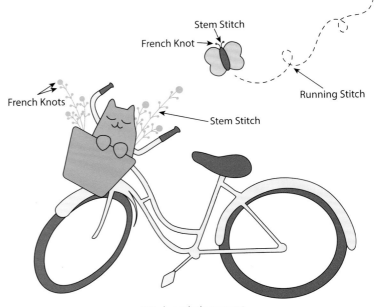

Stitch and placement

4 Referring to Free-Motion Embroidery on Your Domestic Sewing Machine (page 18), stitch around the edges of all the appliqué motifs. Make sure to stitch the circle in the center of the back tire, as well as where the pedal meets the bike. Free-motion embroider the spokes in each wheel using the quilt photo as a guide.

5 Transfer the embroidery designs using your desired method, referring to the stitch and placement diagram. Complete the embroidery.

Make the Patchwork Sections

1 Using a design wall or flat surface, arrange the print squares and triangles for the inner patchwork sections. For each, use 10 squares 3½″ × 3½″ and 5 triangles 3⅞″ × 3⅞″ arranged in 4 rows. Sew the squares and triangles into rows. Press the seams of each row in opposite directions. Join the rows, nesting the seams. Press. Make 4 sections.

2 Arrange the print squares and triangles for the outer patchwork sections. For each, use 10 squares 6½″ × 6½″ and 5 triangles 6⅞″ × 6⅞″ arranged in 4 rows. Sew the squares and triangles in the same manner as the inner patchwork sections. Make 4 sections.

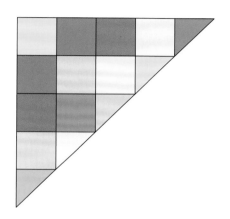

Assemble the Quilt Top

Throughout the assembly process, press the seams toward the pink triangles.

1 Using a design wall or a large flat surface, arrange the patchwork sections and the pink print 1 and pink print 2 quarter-square triangles as shown.

2 Center and sew the pink print 1 triangles to the opposite sides of the center linen square. Press. Center and sew the remaining pink print 1 triangles to the top and bottom of the center linen square. Press.

3 Sew the inner patchwork sections to the quilt center in the same manner. Repeat with the pink print 2 triangles and the outer patchwork sections.

Quilt top assembly

Finishing

Layer the backing, batting, and quilt top. Baste and quilt as desired. Finish with a label and binding.

Whisker Away

Enlarge 200%. Note that the flower sprays have not been reversed in order to use them as embroidery patterns.

Ziggy Kitty Quilt

FINISHED QUILT: 62″ × 74″

This beautifully whimsical quilt was originally designed for my cat-loving daughter's softly-vintage bedroom, which explains why it's a detour from my typically bold, bright designs. The ditsy floral prints and soft pastel colors would seem right at home in a child's bedroom or in any residence where shabby chic style prevails. A more modern version of this quilt might feature bright solids set on an Essex linen background. Whatever your style, give Ziggy Kitty *a try!*

MATERIALS

WHITE SOLID: 3¼ yards for background and inner border

SMALL-SCALE PRINTS: 20 fat quarters for blocks

LIGHT PINK FLORAL: 1½ yards for outer border

BINDING: ⅝ yard

BATTING: 70″ × 82″

BACKING: 4 yards (pieced crosswise) or 4½ yards (pieced lengthwise)

Pieced by Pamela Jane Morgan and Jana Hamilton,
quilted by Kaitlyn Howell (@knotandthread)

Cutting

Note I recommend cutting and sewing one Cat block at a time. Each ziggy block contains many tiny pieces that could become quite overwhelming if cutting out all the blocks at once. I suggest storing each block in a labeled, resealable bag until ready to use.

For each Ziggy Kitty block

WHITE SOLID

- Cut 3 strips 1½″ × width of fabric; subcut into 14 rectangles 2½″ × 1½″, 37 squares 1½″ × 1½″, and 1 rectangle 1½″ × 12½″.
- Cut 1 rectangle 5½″ × 2½″.
- Cut 1 rectangle 4½″ × 5″.
- Cut 1 rectangle 3½″ × 6″.
- Cut 1 rectangle 2½″ × 4½″.
- Cut 4 squares 2¼″ × 2¼″.
- Cut 2 squares 1¾″ × 1¾″.
- Cut 1 square 1″ × 1″.

SMALL-SCALE PRINT

- Cut 2 rectangles 4½″ × 1½″.
- Cut 16 rectangles 2½″ × 1½″.
- Cut 4 squares 2¼″ × 2¼″.
- Cut 2 squares 2″ × 2″.
- Cut 1 square 1¾″ × 1¾″.
- Cut 1 rectangle 1½″ × 2″.
- Cut 28 squares 1½″ × 1½″.

For each print Kitty block

WHITE SOLID

- Cut 1 strip 2½″ × width of fabric; subcut into 1 rectangle 5½″ × 2½″, 1 rectangle 2½″ × 4½″, and 1 square 2½″ × 2½″.
- Cut 1 strip 1½″ × width of fabric; subcut into 1 rectangle 1½″ × 12½″ and 3 squares 1½″ × 1½″.
- Cut 1 rectangle 4½″ × 5″.
- Cut 1 rectangle 3½″ × 6″.

SMALL-SCALE PRINT

- Cut 1 rectangle 5½″ × 10½″.
- Cut 2 rectangles 4½″ × 1½″.
- Cut 1 rectangle 2½″ × 8½″.
- Cut 2 squares 2″ × 2″.
- Cut 1 rectangle 1½″ × 6″.

Inner border

WHITE SOLID

- Cut 6 strips 2″ × width of fabric.

Outer border

LIGHT PINK FLORAL

- Cut 7 strips 6″ × width of fabric.

Binding

- Cut 8 strips 2¼″ × width of fabric.

Construction

Make the Ziggy Kitty Blocks

Press all seam allowances open unless otherwise specified.

MAKE THE CHEVRON UNITS

CHEVRON A

1 For each chevron A unit, use 1 print rectangle 2½″ × 1½″ and 2 white squares 1½″ × 1½″. Follow the instructions for Stitch-and-Flip Flying Geese (page 9).

2 Make 14 chevron A units for *each* Ziggy Kitty block. **A**

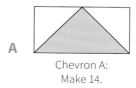

A

Chevron A:
Make 14.

CHEVRON B

1 For each chevron B unit, use 1 white rectangle 2½″ × 1½″ and 2 print squares 1½″ × 1½″. Follow the instructions for Stitch-and-Flip Flying Geese (page 9).

2 Make 14 chevron B units for *each* Ziggy Kitty block. **B**

B

Chevron B:
Make 14.

CHEVRON C

1 For each chevron C unit, use 1 print square 2¼″ × 2¼″ and 1 white square 2¼″ × 2¼″. Follow the instructions for Two-at-a-Time Stitch-and-Flip Piecing (page 9).

2 Cut the squares in half on the drawn line to make 2 units. Trim each chevron C unit to 1½″ × 1½″ (see Square It Up, page 10). Make 8 chevron C units for *each* Ziggy Kitty block. **C**

C

Chevron C:
Make 8.

CHEVRON D

1 For each chevron D unit, use 1 print square 1¾″ × 1¾″ and 1 white square 1¾″ × 1¾″. Follow the instructions for Stitch-and-Flip Piecing (page 8) to make a half-square triangle unit.

2 Draw a diagonal line on the wrong side of an additional white square 1¾″ × 1¾″. Place the half-square triangle unit right side up with the print on the left. Place the white square on top, right sides together, with the drawn line perpendicular to the previous seam. Sew on the drawn line. Trim, leaving ¼″ seam allowance. Trim the chevron D unit to 1½″ × 1½″ (see Square It Up, page 10). Make 1 chevron D unit for *each* Ziggy Kitty block. **D**

D

Chevron D:
Make 1.

MAKE THE CAT HEAD

① Make the ear unit using 1 white rectangle 5½″ × 2½″ and 2 print squares 2″ × 2″. Follow the instructions for Stitch-and-Flip Piecing (page 8). **E**

② For row 1, sew together 2 chevron A and 1 chevron C units.

③ For row 2, sew together 2 chevron B and 1 chevron C units.

④ Join the rows. The ear unit is on top, followed by row 1 and row 2.

⑤ Sew 1 white rectangle 2½″ × 4½″ to the right edge of the joined rows to complete the cat head unit. **F**

MAKE THE BODY UNIT

① For row 1 of the body unit, sew together 3 chevron A units and 1 white square 1½″ × 1½″.

② For row 2, sew together 3 chevron B and 1 chevron D units. The print section of the chevron D unit should align with the print section of the adjacent chevron B unit.

③ For rows 3, 5, and 7, sew together 3 chevron A and 1 chevron C units for each row.

④ For rows 4, 6, and 8, sew together 3 chevron B and 1 chevron C units for each row.

⑤ Join rows 1–8 in order.

⑥ Sew together the cat head and body units. **G**

MAKE THE TAIL UNIT

① Make the tail top unit, using 2 white squares 1½″ × 1½″ and 1 print rectangle 4½″ × 1½″. Follow the instructions for Stitch-and-Flip Piecing (page 8). **H**

② The tail middle unit features a striped tail section. For stripe unit A, use 1 print rectangle 1½″ × 2″, 1 white square 1″ × 1″, and 1 white square 1½″ × 1½″. Draw a diagonal line on the wrong side of both white squares.

E

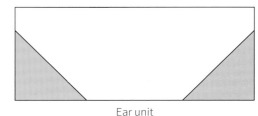

Ear unit

F

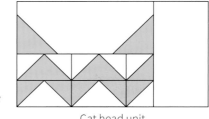

Cat head unit

G

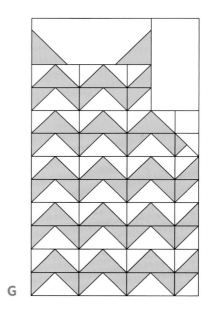

H

Tail top unit

3 Place the marked white square 1″ × 1″ on the top left corner of the print rectangle. Sew on the drawn line and then trim the seam allowance to ¼″. Repeat on bottom right corner using the other marked white square 1½″ × 1½″. Make 1 unit. **I**

4 For stripe unit B, use 1 print rectangle 2½″ × 1½″ and 2 white squares 1½″ × 1½″. Follow the instructions for Stitch-and-Flip Piecing (page 8). Make 2 units. **J**

5 Sew together the stripe units in a column, with stripe unit A on top. The stripes should run parallel to one another. With right sides together, sew the striped tail section to 1 white rectangle 3½″ × 6″ to complete the tail middle unit.

6 Make the tail bottom unit, using 1 white square 1½″ × 1½″ and 1 print rectangle 4½″ × 1½″. Follow the instructions for Stitch-and-Flip Piecing (page 8). **K**

7 Assemble the tail unit, sewing a white rectangle 4½″ × 5″ to the top. **L**

FINISH THE ZIGGY KITTY BLOCKS

1 Join the body and tail units.

2 Sew 1 white rectangle 1½″ × 12½″ to the left edge of the joined units.

3 Make 10 Ziggy Kitty blocks. Each block should measure 12½″ × 12½″ including seam allowances (12″ × 12″ finished). **M**

I

Stripe unit A: Make 1.

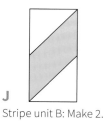
J

Stripe unit B: Make 2.

K

Tail bottom unit

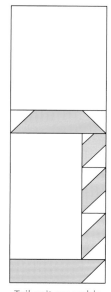
L

Tail unit assembly

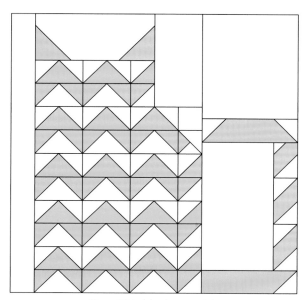
M

Ziggy Kitty block assembly

Make the Print Kitty Blocks

Press all seams open for this block.

1 Use the print Kitty block assembly diagram as a guide for placement. For detailed piecing instructions, see One Cat Leads to Another (page 10).

Note This cat block differs from the other cat blocks because there isn't a half-square triangle in the bottom left corner of the body unit.

2 Finish each print Kitty block by sewing a white rectangle 1½″ × 12½″ to the left edge of the block.

3 Make 10 print Kitty blocks. Each block should measure 12½″ × 12½″ including seam allowances (12″ × 12″ finished). **N**

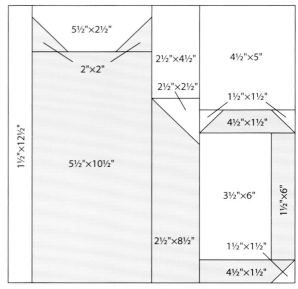

Print Kitty block assembly

Make the Inner Border

1 Sew the white strips 2″ × width of fabric together end to end. Press the seams open.

2 Subcut into 2 strips 2″ × 60½″ for the side borders and 2 strips 2″ × 51½″ for the top and bottom borders.

Make the Outer Border

1 Sew the pink strips 6″ × width of fabric together end to end. Press the seams open.

2 Subcut into 2 strips 6″ × 63½″ for the side borders and 2 strips 6″ × 62½″ for the top and bottom borders.

Assemble the Quilt Top

1 Referring to quilt photo, arrange the blocks in 5 rows of 4 blocks each, alternating Ziggy Kitty blocks and print Kitty blocks. Experiment with the arrangement of blocks to ensure even color distribution throughout.

2 Sew the blocks into rows. Press the seams in opposite directions. Join the rows, nesting the seams together. Press.

3 Sew the white inner border strips to the sides of the quilt top. Press the seams to the borders. Sew the white inner border strips to the top and bottom of the quilt top. Press the seams to the borders.

4 Sew the pink outer border strips to the sides of the quilt top. Press the seams to the pink borders. Sew the pink outer border strips to the top and bottom of the quilt top. Press the seams to the pink borders.

Finishing

Layer the backing, batting, and quilt top. Baste and quilt as desired. Finish with a label and binding.

Quilt top assembly

Laser Cat Quilt

FINISHED QUILT: 72″ × 78″

Remember how I mentioned that I've made quilts that were designed based on fabric that was too purr-fect to cut up? This quilt is one of them! Cats in space suits appealed to my nerdy sensibility and also reminded me of one of my favorite late-night comedy skits. My husband and I agree to disagree when it comes to late-night sketch comedy, but one thing we both can't help but laugh over is cats who shoot laser beams from their eyes. This quilt is both beginner-friendly and scrap-friendly, and the fun rainbow effect comes from clever fabric placement. Whether or not you're a fan of sketch comedy, you're sure to be a fan of this pawesome quilt!

MATERIALS

NAVY PRINTS: 20 fat quarters

WHITE SOLID: ¼ yard for eyes

BLACK SOLID: ¼ yard for eyes and nose

RED PRINTS: ⅓ yard total of assorted scraps

ORANGE PRINTS: ½ yard total of assorted scraps

YELLOW PRINTS: ½ yard total of assorted scraps

GREEN PRINTS: ½ yard total of assorted scraps

TURQUOISE PRINTS: ½ yard total of assorted scraps

PURPLE PRINTS: ½ yard total of assorted scraps

HOT PINK PRINTS: ⅓ yard total of assorted scraps

BINDING: ⅝ yard of rainbow stripe print

BACKING: 5 yards

BATTING: 80″ × 86″

Cutting

Navy prints

- Cut 6 squares 6½″ × 6½″ from *each* of 16 fat quarters.
- Cut 2 squares 6¾″ × 6¾″ from *each* of 4 fat quarters.

White solid

- Cut 2 rectangles 6½″ × 12½″.
- Cut 2 squares 6½″ × 6½″.

Black solid

- Cut 1 rectangle 6½″ × 12½″.
- Cut 2 squares 6½″ × 6½″.

Red prints

- Cut 4 squares 6¾″ × 6¾″.
- Cut 2 squares 6½″ × 6½″.

Orange prints

- Cut 8 squares 6½″ × 6½″.

Yellow prints

- Cut 8 squares 6½″ × 6½″.

Green prints

- Cut 8 squares 6½″ × 6½″.

Turquoise prints

- Cut 8 squares 6½″ × 6½″.

Purple prints

- Cut 2 squares 6¾″ × 6¾″.
- Cut 6 squares 6½″ × 6½″.

Hot pink prints

- Cut 2 squares 6¾″ × 6¾″.
- Cut 4 squares 6½″ × 6½″.

Binding

- Cut 9 strips 2¼″ × width of fabric.

Pieced by Pamela Jane Morgan
and Charisma Horton, quilted by
Rob Dickinson (@roboquilter)

Construction

Piece the Face Units

1 For the left eye, sew 1 white square 6½″ × 6½″ and 1 black square 6½″ × 6½″ together. Press the seam to the black square. Sew to 1 white rectangle 6½″ × 12½″. Press toward the pieced row. **A**

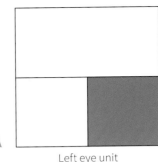

A

Left eye unit

2 For the right eye, sew 1 white square 6½″ × 6½″, 1 black square 6½″ × 6½″, and 1 white rectangle 6½″ × 12½″ rectangle together as in Step 1, except arrange the squares so the black square is to the left. **B**

3 For the nose, use the black rectangle 6½″ × 12½″ and 2 assorted turquoise squares 6½″ × 6½″. Follow the instructions for Stitch-And-Flip Flying Geese (page 9). **C**

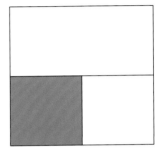

B

Right eye unit

Make the Ear Units

1 Select 4 navy print squares 6¾″ × 6¾″ and 4 red print squares 6¾″ × 6¾″. Draw a diagonal line on the wrong side of the red print squares.

2 Layer each red print square with a navy print square, right sides together. Following the instructions for stitch-and-flip piecing (page 8), make 4 half-square triangle units.

3 Trim each half-square triangle unit to 6½″ × 6½″ square (see Square it Up, page 10). **D**

C

Nose unit

Make the Remaining Half-Square Triangle Units

1 Select 4 navy print squares 6¾″ × 6¾″, 2 purple print squares 6¾″ × 6¾″, and 2 hot pink squares 6¾″ × 6¾″. Draw a diagonal line on the wrong side of the purple and pink squares.

2 Layer each purple square and each pink square with a navy square, right sides together. Following the instructions for stitch-and-flip piecing (page 8), make 2 purple half-square triangles and 2 pink half-square triangles.

3 Trim each half-square triangle to 6½″ × 6½″. **E**

D

Ear unit: Make 4.

E

Make 2.   Make 2.

Quilt top assembly

Assemble the Quilt Top

1 Using a design wall or large flat surface, arrange the squares and half-square triangle units into 13 rows of 12 squares/units each.

2 Sew the squares and units into rows. Press the seams of each row in alternating directions.

3 Join the rows, nesting the seams together. Press the seams in one direction.

Finishing

Layer the backing, batting, and quilt top. Baste and quilt as desired. Finish with a label and binding.

Backing fabric designed by Rae Ritchie for Dear Stella Fabrics

Chasing Dreams Quilt

FINISHED QUILT: 60″ × 72″

Chasing Dreams is a visual representation of what I imagine kitties daydreaming about. I picture my own kitties, dreaming about chasing bees and butterflies in fields of flowers, or chasing a giant ball of yarn. This row-by-row quilt features four rows of appliquéd kitties and flowers plus two yarn balls made from real yarn. The four rows of appliqué are separated by rows of scrappy flying geese blocks. While these blocks appear complicated, they're simplified by using the eight-at-a-time half-square triangle (HST) method. I chose flying geese blocks because my cats' favorite pastime is staring out our large picture windows at all the birds that inhabit our backyard. The quilt is finished with wavy top and bottom edges, which symbolize the sometimes-blurred line between fantasy and reality.

MATERIALS

NOTE: *Get ready to raid your scrap bin! With the exception of the appliqué background requirement, all prints are listed with the number and size of squares needed instead of yardage amounts. This will give your quilt a truly scrappy appearance, and—bonus—it's a great way to use up orphaned precuts.*

Low-volume prints

½ yard *each* of 7 prints for appliqué background

24 squares 6″ × 6″

90 squares 2½″ × 2½″

Blue prints

6 squares 6″ × 6″

24 squares 2½″ × 2½″

Turquoise prints

6 squares 6″ × 6″

24 squares 2½″ × 2½″

Chartreuse prints

6 squares 6″ × 6″

24 squares 2½″ × 2½″

Green prints

6 squares 6″ × 6″

24 squares 2½″ × 2½″

Wool-blend felt

KELLY: 12″ × 18″ piece for cats

SEAFOAM: 12″ × 18″ piece for cats

MARINE: ½ yard for cats and flowers

POOL: ½ yard for cats and flowers

JULEP: 9″ × 12″ piece for flowers

ZUCCHINI: 6″ × 9″ piece for stems and leaves

MEADOW: 6″ × 9″ piece for stems and leaves

Hand-dyed wool

SCRAPS IN A VARIETY OF SIZES AND COORDINATING COLORS for details

Binding

1⅛ yards

Backing

4½ yards

Batting

68″ × 80″

Additional materials

PAPER-BACKED FUSIBLE WEB: 3 yards, 20″ wide

COORDINATING 6-STRAND EMBROIDERY FLOSS OR SIZE 8 PERLE COTTON

COORDINATING SKEIN OF YARN

TEMPLATE PLASTIC

Pieced and appliquéd by Pamela Jane Morgan, quilted
and couched by Charisma Horton (@charismahorton)

Cutting

Low-volume prints

- Cut 1 strip 12½″ × width of fabric from *each* of 7 low-volume prints; subcut *each* into 3 squares 12½″ × 12½″.
- *Optional:* Cut additional squares 6″ × 6″ and 2½″ × 2½″ from the remainder for scrappier Flying Geese blocks.

Binding

- Cut 1 square 36″ × 36″.

Construction

Piecing

APPLIQUÉ BACKGROUND

Sew 5 low-volume squares 12½″ × 12½″ into a row. Press the seams *open* to create a nice, flat background for the appliqué. Make 4 rows. (There will be 1 square leftover.)

SCRAPPY FLYING GEESE

1 Pair 1 low-volume square 6″ × 6″ with 1 print square 6″ × 6″. Following the instructions for eight-at-a-time half-square triangles (next page), create 48 half-square triangle units in *each* of the 4 colorways (blue, turquoise, chartreuse, and green).

2 Assemble the Flying Geese blocks by colorway. Arrange 2 low-volume print squares 2½″ × 2½″, 2 print squares 2½″ × 2½″, and 4 half-square triangle units for each Flying Geese block. Sew into 2 rows. Press the seams in opposite directions. Join the rows, nesting the seams. Press.

3 Make 45 Flying Geese blocks. You will need 12 blocks in one colorway and 11 blocks of each of the remaining 3 colorways. Assemble the Flying Geese blocks into 3 rows of 15 blocks each. Press. Note that I used the colors in sequence, giving some order to the scrappiness.

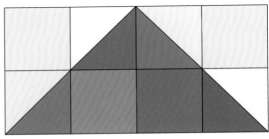

Flying Geese block assembly

EIGHT-AT-A-TIME HALF-SQUARE TRIANGLES

Each scrappy Flying Geese block requires 4 half-square triangle units. With 45 Flying Geese blocks, the time really begins to add up! To save time, we'll make our half-square triangles 8 at a time.

1. For each set of 8 half-square triangles, you'll need 1 low-volume print square 6″ × 6″ and 1 print square 6″ × 6″ from one of the 4 colorways.

2. Draw 2 diagonal lines on the wrong side of the low-volume print square.

3. Sew ¼″ seams on each side of the diagonal lines. **A**

4. Using your rotary cutter, cut the block in half lengthwise. **B**

5. Now cut the block in half widthwise. **C**

6. Cut on both diagonal lines. **D**

7. Press the triangles open. Trim each half-square triangle unit to 2½″ × 2½″ (see Square It Up, page 10).

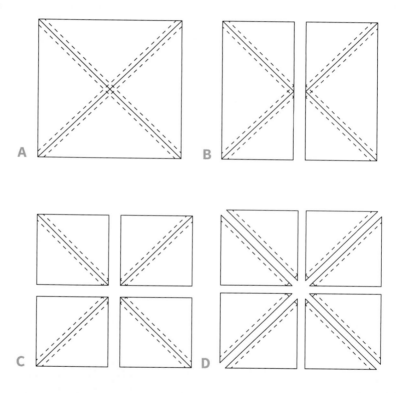

Appliqué and Embroidery

1 Enlarge the appliqué patterns (pages 139–143) to 200%, if noted on the patterns. Trace on paper-backed fusible web. Trace 2 each of cat patterns A, B, and C. Trace 1 each of cat patterns D and Dr (D reversed). Trace 2 each of the remaining appliqué shapes, unless noted differently on the patterns. Cut and fuse to the wool and felt pieces, referring to Raw-Edge Appliqué (page 22).

2 Arrange the appliqué motifs on the pieced background, referring to the quilt photo (next page). Fuse and then stitch in place either by hand or machine.

3 Transfer the embroidery designs using your desired method. Complete the embroidery.

TIP *The appliqué elements in this quilt were attached using a combination of hand and machine stitches. To make this quilt uniquely yours, experiment with both hand and machine decorative stitches beforehand to see if what looks best suits your vision. Then apply your favorites to this quilt!*

STITCH SUGGESTIONS

1 Sew the cats' bodies to the background using a straight stitch a scant ⅛″ from the edges.

2 Stitch the faces using all 6 strands of embroidery floss and a backstitch. Repeat, making a second row of backstitching, to make the faces extra visible.

3 Attach the flowers using a straight stitch. Embellish the flower centers with French knots. For the stems, sew a single straight stitch down the center of each stem.

4 Use hidden whipstitches to attach small pieces such as the bee and butterfly.

Assemble the Quilt Top

1 Arrange and sew the appliquéd rows and the Flying Geese rows together. Pay careful attention to which direction the Flying Geese are facing when joining the rows.

2 Make the yarn ball using yarn and a couching stitch (page 17). Alternatively, if you are sending your quilt to a longarm quilter, you can ask if they are capable of couching the yarn.

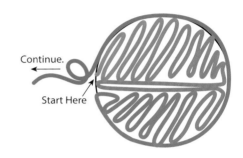

Finishing

1 Layer the backing, batting, and quilt top. Baste and quilt as desired. Finish with a label and binding.

2 Enlarge and trace the wavy edge pattern (page 143) onto template plastic and cut out along the traced lines. Using a water-soluble marker, trace the template along the top left block of the quilt, aligning the curve with the top edge. Mark the curve. Move to the next block, flipping the template upside down so that straight edge aligns to top of quilt. Mark the curve. Repeat for the remainder of the top edge of the quilt; then repeat on the bottom edge of the quilt. Using sharp fabric scissors, trim the quilt along the marked wavy lines.

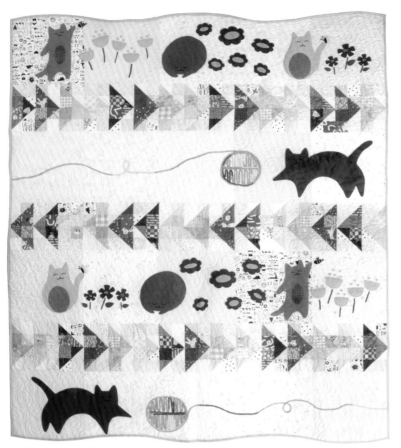

Quilt top assembly

3 Use the binding fabric square 36″ × 36″ to make 2½″-wide continuous bias binding (see Continuous Bias Binding, page 26). Bind the quilt, carefully following the wavy edges. Label as desired.

TIP *Take care not to stretch the binding when you are stitching it to the curved edges. When bias binding is stretched, it can cause the edges of the quilt to curl.*

HANDIWORK

I left the couching of the yarn ball on my quilt to a purr-fessional. But what if you're not planning on sending your *Chasing Dreams* quilt to a longarmer?

Check out this gorgeous pink and purple version of *Chasing Dreams*, made by Sherri Noel (Rebecca Mae Designs). She couched her yarn by hand and it is absolutely stunning!

Chasing Dreams, pieced, quilted, and couched by Sherri Noel (@rebeccamaedesigns)

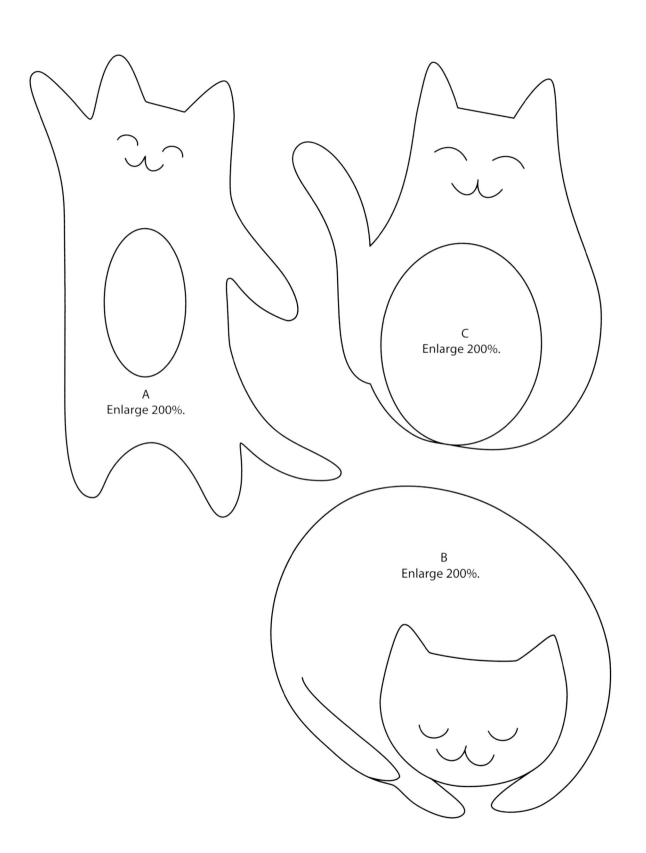

A
Enlarge 200%.

C
Enlarge 200%.

B
Enlarge 200%.

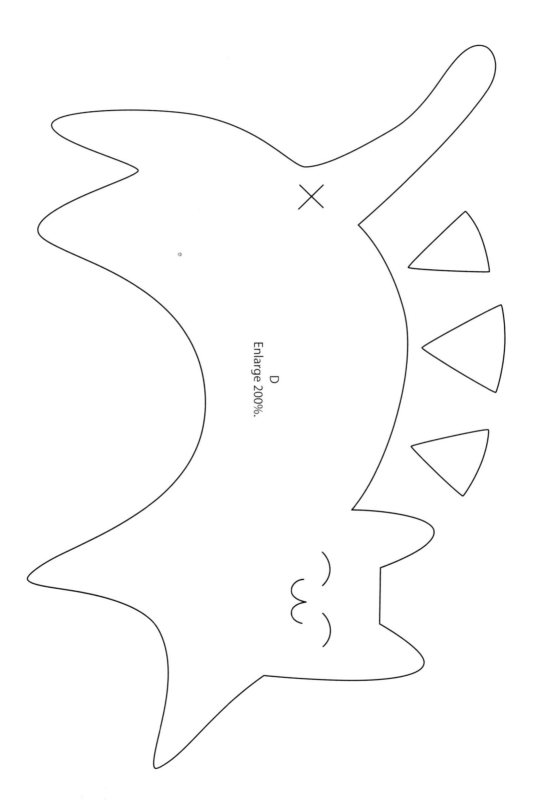

D
Enlarge 200%.

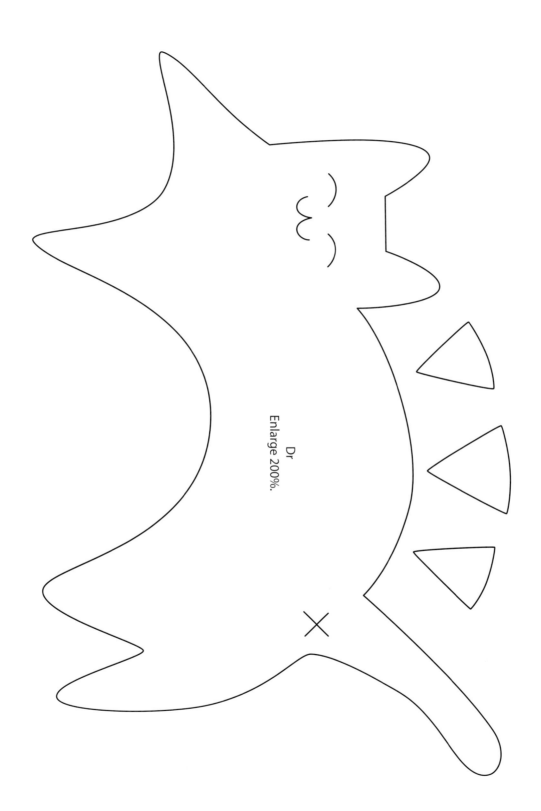

Dr
Enlarge 200%.

Flower Set F: Cut 2.

Flower Set E: Cut 10.

Flower Set F: Cut 4.

Flower Set F: Cut 4.

Flower Set F: Cut 2.

Yarn Ball
Enlarge 200%.

Flower Set G: Cut 2.

Flower Set G: Cut 2.

Flower Set G: Cut 2.

Wavy Edge
Enlarge 200%.

Butterfly

Bee

About the Author

PAMELA JANE MORGAN is an award-winning quilter and photographer. She is also a crazy cat lady! Pamela comes from a long line of sewists and artists, and began quilting as a creative outlet while pregnant with her first child. Becoming a mother also inspired her to become a photographer. She draws her inspiration from the world around her, especially from her cats. While working in the photography industry, Pamela quickly discovered she could sneak her passion for quilting into her photos. Her work has been featured in magazines, such as *Quilting Quickly*; local and regional quilt shows; and the Moda Bake Shop. She lives on a farm in Idaho Falls, Idaho, with her husband, four children, and a small menagerie that includes four cats.

Visit Pamela online and follow on social media!

Website: pammiejane.com

Pinterest: /pammiejane

Instagram: @pammiejane

Photo by Emily Downey